Students and Teachers of the New China

Thirteen Interviews

MADELYN HOLMES

McFarland & Company, Inc., Publishers

Jefferson, North Carolina, and London

LIBRARY OF CONGRESS CATALOGUING-IN-PUBLICATION DATA

Holmes, Madelyn, 1945–
    Students and teachers of the new China : thirteen interviews /
by Madelyn Holmes.
        p.   cm.
    Includes bibliographical references and index.

    ISBN-13: 978-0-7864-3288-2
    softcover : 50# alkaline paper ∞
                                    1007240255

    1. Teachers — China — Interviews.   2. Teachers — China —
Social conditions.   3. Students — China — Interviews.
4. Students — China — Social conditions.   I. Title.
LA2383.C5H73   2008
371.100951— dc22   2007027614

British Library cataloguing data are available

Cover photograph ©2007 Shutterstock

Manufactured in the United States of America

McFarland & Company, Inc., Publishers
  Box 611, Jefferson, North Carolina 28640
    www.mcfarlandpub.com

Table of Contents

Map   vi

Preface   1

Introduction   5

PART ONE: STUDENTS   29

1. Urban Undergraduates Born in the 1980s   33

2. Rural Students Born in the 1980s   57

3. An Xin, Born in the 1980s   83

PART TWO: TEACHERS   103

4. Born in the 1970s   107

5. Born in the 1960s and 1950s   130

PART THREE: FACES OF THE FUTURE   151

6. Born in the 1990s   155

7. Conclusion   174

Bibliography   197

Index   199

Hometowns of 13 interviewees: 1. Evelyn (ch 1): Hangzhou; 2. William (ch 1): Shanghai; 3. Sunnie (ch 1): Beijing; 4. Vivian (ch 1): Zhengzhou; 5. Wendy (ch 2): Sai hui village; 6. Fan Gao (ch 2): Sankou; 7. Xue Yan (ch 2): Wangdianzi village; 8. An Xin (ch 3): Xianyang; 9. Shirley (ch 4): Shaoxing; 10. Shao Bin (ch 4): Zhujia village; 11. Alice (ch 4): Yuhuan county; 12. Professor Chen (ch 5): Lanzhou; 13. Ian (ch 5): Ningbo.

Preface

I have returned in this book to writing history in much the same manner as in *American Women Conservationists* (McFarland, 2004), which featured profiles of twelve women who had devoted their lives to protecting the natural environment of the United States. In both books, biographies of individuals provide a lens through which to understand historical developments. Here I explore the contemporary history of China, observing the impact of headline-grabbing events on the lives of Chinese people.

I interviewed thirteen Chinese students and teachers who were living in Hangzhou, a major city in south central China situated only two hours by train from Shanghai. This book tells their real-life stories. Born in the 1950s, 1960s, 1970s, 1980s, or 1990s, at the time of the interviews they ranged in age from 11 to 52. None was alive at the founding of the People's Republic of China in 1949, but many of the parents and grandparents whose lives they described witnessed the entire course of events from 1949 to 2005. I chose to use the name New China in the book's title because, as the country's nickname, it reflects the aspirations as well as the realities of this nation, which is creating itself anew.

My entrée to China was an appointment as visiting professor of English at Zhejiang University in Hangzhou, made possible through the invitation of Professor Dr. Ulrich Steinmueller, then dean of the School of International Studies. This all sounds straightforward and well-planned — in contrast to the way it actually happened.

When I began to consider teaching English at a Chinese university, I took out a map of China and drew a line that corresponded to the course of the Yangtze River. Because my home is in Burlington, Vermont, in the far north of the United States, I wanted to find a university in China in a place with a much warmer climate. I consulted a directory of world universities and narrowed in on Nanjing, Suzhou, Shanghai, and Hangzhou. Previously I had taught writing and history at universities in Washington, D.C., and Cambridge, Massachusetts, as well as in Ottawa, Canada, and in England at Cambridge and at the University of East Anglia in Norwich, where I received a doctoral degree in history.

Via the Internet I sent out letters and my curriculum vitae to Chinese professors of English, but received no replies. During the long winter of 2004 I looked again at the Website for Zhejiang University in Hangzhou. To my amazement I read that Dr. Steinmueller of Berlin, Germany, had been appointed the first foreign dean of a Chinese university. Immediately, I wrote an email message addressed to him and he responded. After negotiations that continued for several months I received my offer of a teaching position in June.

Everyone interviewed for this book had a connection to education, as either a student or a teacher, and the phrase "key school" occurs repeatedly in the text. Located in cities and towns throughout China, key schools have special significance, for they serve as model schools or universities. They have the most modern facilities and the best-trained teachers. Zhejiang University is a key university, and many of my students attended key schools before beginning university education.

The names of the interviewees in this book are names that I personally have received permission to publish. Some interviewees agreed to use their Chinese names and others preferred English names to retain anonymity. All the interviewees spoke fluent English, and each had taken an English name at some time during his or her English language studies. In Chinese usage, the surnames of both women and men are written first; Professor Chen (see chapter 5), however, preferred to use the English order with her given name written first. Customarily in China, married women do not assume their husband's surname, but retain their own family name. A child takes the father's surname.

The writing of this book depended upon the cooperation of the thirteen Chinese people whose life stories comprise the body of the text. I am indebted to each person for sharing personal history and in several cases for introducing me to family members. I am especially grateful to Evelyn for arranging a delicious dinner with her parents, and to Sunnie for the traditional Chinese meal and personal tour of Beijing and for the two occasions when I was able to become acquainted with her mother. Special thanks to William, who guided us on a personalized tour of Shanghai and wrote up his interview with his mother. Special thanks to Vivian, who wrote up her interview with her parents and grandmother. Special thanks to Xue Yan, who wrote up her interview with her grandmother. In particular, I want to thank Fan Gao and his extended family for welcoming me into their households and for showing me faces of rural China. I express my deeply felt gratitude to my English department colleague Ian, whose hospitality to me in Hangzhou and willingness to arrange visits to a school, library, and to a historic village not only enriched my understanding of China but also created a strong bond of friendship. On December 31, 2005, my husband and I greeted the new year at a Chinese restaurant in Hangzhou with nine of the participants in this book, all of whom have become our genuine friends.

In addition to the people interviewed I want to thank other Chinese teachers and students at Zhejiang University whom we got to know well and who related tales of their lives. Special thanks to Professor Longhai Xiao of the college of education for arranging for my school visits to Deqing Vocational School and to Daguan Middle School. Also, I want to thank non–Chinese friends, especially my fellow foreign experts who shared a small, fourth-floor office in the School of International Studies, and my neighbors on the Yuquan campus, who shared insights about life in China.

I want to thank Brooke Carleton of Burlington, Vermont, for drawing the map of China and Christophe Agou of New York City for contributing his photograph of An Xin. My husband, Lewis, not only accompanied me to China but relished every minute there. As a fellow author, he critically read the manuscript and marked it up with his famous red pen, for which I am sincerely grateful. My mother, Barbara Berch Jamison, died before this book was published, but I will appreciate forever her encouragement to me, her enthusiasm for living productively, and her sincere interest in following what was happening in China.

My final thank-you is to An Xin, whose emotional attachment to my family has helped to cement a connection between myself and China that will last a lifetime. Thank you for your honesty, accessibility, warmth, and passion for life.

Introduction

The most pervasive impression I brought back from my one year of teaching in Hangzhou, China, can be encapsulated in one word: CHANGE. Every day, every person, every place I saw was in perpetual motion. That of course refers to all the new things — houses, shops, parks, roads, plants, fountains — that altered the way that streets, buildings, neighborhoods, and city centers look. But change extended beyond what I could see with my naked eye. The transformation of Chinese society affects the daily lives of every Chinese person, causing continual adjustments to ways of eating, dressing, housing, learning, working, recreating and thinking.

Before I arrived in China in February 2005 I had decided that my research project would focus on New China, illuminating historical events that have taken place there between 1949 and 2005 by interviewing people between the ages of ten and ninety. I would piece together a real-life history of New China from individual personal stories. But how was I to identify these "faces of New China"? As a visiting professor of English at Zhejiang University in Hangzhou, I met students who were in their twenties. These twenty-somethings introduced me to their parents and in one case to a grandparent. I also met their teachers, who were my colleagues and who were in their thirties, forties and fifties.

These biographies of Chinese people are the stories of my friends, because from the first day when my husband and I were welcomed at the Hangzhou train station by Brenda, a bright senior who spoke fluent English, we were befriended. Everyone wanted to make our acquaintance, and we in fact made more friends than we ever had before in our more than sixty years.

I met two generations of many Chinese families: several parents of university students and several children of university professors. Three students researched their family backgrounds, and in their cases I was able to document three generations: eight decades of Chinese history beginning in the 1930s.

The China I observed in the year 2005 was "brimming with vigor and vitality" in the words of Wen Jiabao, who has been the country's premier since 2003. When Hu Jintao, China's president and general secretary of the Communist Party, visited the United States in April 2006 he may have impressed students and professors at Yale University, whom he addressed, with China's spectacular economic statistics, in particular its GDP that rose from $147.3 billion in 1978 to $2.2 trillion in 2005. But he also stressed that "China remains the world's largest developing country ... with daunting challenges in its development endeavor." This impressive gross national income translates into a per capita annual income of only $1,730. Wen Jiabao and Hu Jintao, the fourth generation of politicians to govern the People's Republic of China since its founding in 1949, are leading a country with more than twenty-five years of experience in opening up its economy to the world market, and they are building upon the previous success of raising 200 million Chinese out of poverty and into a relatively comfortable standard of living. Yet, as the Chinese premier often says, "Any considerable amount of financial and material resources divided by 1.3 billion becomes a very low per capita level. This is a reality the Chinese leaders have to keep firmly in mind at all times."

Another reality of contemporary China is the disparity in levels of prosperity among regions of the country and between urban and rural areas. My vantage point was a southern, coastal urban area, the Yangtze River Delta. Hangzhou, the city I lived in, is the capital of Zhejiang province, one of the most prosperous of China's twenty-three provinces,* and the metropolis of booming Shanghai is only 112 miles away. The growth of a market economy in this region occurred much earlier than in western and more inland areas of the country, and in discussions of China's income gap Zhejiang province is near the top of the list of rich versus poor provinces.

According to the Chinese government, Taiwan is a province of China.

City of Hangzhou

In the late thirteenth century, Marco Polo called Hangzhou "paradise on earth," and in 2005 his hyperbolic sobriquet still fits, though marred by many of the familiar problems that confront large cities in the twenty-first century. From my first view out of the taxi window, en route to my Zhejiang University digs from the main train station, to my last view out of the long-distance bus that returned me to Shanghai's Pudong airport, the city lived up to its nickname.

With an urban population of four million, plus the two million more who live in the surrounding suburbs, the city enjoys aspects of paradise: a famous lake, green hills, broad river, botanical gardens, fields of Dragon Well tea, modern and traditional shopping streets, historical landmarks, and culture galore. There are museums for silk and tea, Buddhist and Taoist temples, Christian and Moslem shrines, monuments to political figures, hundreds of schools and universities, and so many art galleries, operas, and restaurants to frequent that my one year served only as an introduction to what Hangzhou offers its residents and visitors.

The city is not only a future capital for leisure activities, as it aspires to become, but also functions as the political and economic capital of Zhejiang province. Historically, five categories of industry, namely electronic information, pharmaceutical and chemicals, food and beverages, machinery, and textiles and garments, have formed its manufacturing backbone. But today the hard-to-avoid side effects of economic development, traffic congestion, polluted skies and waters, and blatant dichotomies in living conditions between residents and migrant workers have blemished somewhat Marco Polo's image of an earthly paradise.

The history of Hangzhou can be traced back 2,200 years, but its fame as one of China's seven ancient capitals is of more recent date. From 893 A.D., the city served as the capital of the Wuyue kingdom for eighty years, and then during one hundred and fifty years (1129 to 1279) it reached its pinnacle of prominence as the capital of the Southern Song dynasty. Yet, at least at one other time in Chinese history, the limelight shone on Hangzhou. In 610 A.D., the longest man-made canal in the world, the 1,116 mile-long Grand Canal stretching from Beijing to Hangzhou, was opened for commerce. This water channel made it possible to transport grain from the fertile fields of south China to supply the rice bowls of the north, as well as expediting the trade of salt and silk. Today, water still flows in the Grand Canal but tourists are the principal commerce. In what might be considered a replay of history, the massive South-to-North water diversion project, launched at the end of 2002, envisions construction of three man-made rivers to channel water from southern China to the drought-ridden north. One of these "rivers," the 1,156 kilometer eastern diversion line, will flow along the Grand Canal.

To the popular mind Hangzhou is most renowned for its West Lake, a small but ancient body of water dredged out of a low-lying bay that fed into the East China Sea. It is beautiful, the epitome of the traditional Chinese aesthetic that combines man with nature. I live beside Lake Champlain in Burlington, Vermont, and I had considered that landscape of water surrounded by mountains an ideal scenic site. And it is, but West Lake is different. There are bridges, pagodas, pavilions, fountains, teahouses, and people reveling in pleasure everywhere. They are flying kites, strolling, boating, sipping tea, playing mahjong, being photographed. Others practice singing opera or come together in musical ensembles of erhu, the two-stringed Chinese violin, and bamboo flutes.

West Lake lies in the center of Hangzhou, facing downtown skyscrapers to the east and surrounded by forested hills to the south, north and west. Lakeside villas with their landscaped gardens built by rich merchants and officials are now museums open to the public, and the bright lights that illuminate the hills above West Lake in the evening belong not to individual house owners but are city-operated amenities for everyone's enjoyment. Hangzhou has worked hard to bring West Lake back to its centuries-held reputation. Photographs exhibited in the new lakeside museum illustrate its state of dereliction in 1949 after years of war and civic neglect. Hangzhou's citizens went to work cleaning up the lake in the 1950s, and since then continuous planting of trees, renovations of buildings, and reconstruction of causeways have integrated the artificial features with the natural ingredients to recreate its harmonious Chinese beauty. Into this mix an American architect named Benjamin Wood designed a section of lakeside park along the southern bank, adding international eateries but also renovating old buildings according to western concepts of historical preservation and environmentally sustainable development.

The variety of pleasure boats for hire now include self-operating rowboats and small electric craft as well as the larger antique cruise ships that ply the lake day and night upholding traditional pleasures reminiscent of at least one thousand years ago. Whatever the season and whatever the festival, the gardeners of West Lake plant to fit the occasion: peach blossoms in the spring; lotus flowers in summer; sweet-scented osmanthus in the autumn; and plum blossoms in winter. As I stood on the north bank of the lake between the Bai and Su causeways marveling at the large "lotus leaves swaying in the breeze," the name associated with this vantage point, I was startled by a sign marking this site as one of the "Ten Scenes of West Lake" revered by visitors since the Southern Song Dynasty.

Famous Chinese poets, in particular Bai Juyi and Su Shi (also called Su Dong-po), have helped to spread the reputation of West Lake. During the Tang dynasty, for several years in the early 820s, Bai Juyi served as one of the city's influential governor-poets and was responsible for constructing Bai's dam on West Lake. His output of poems was impressively large and wide-ranging in topics, including not only incidents in daily life but also, as a Confucian poet, judgments about the role of government in people's lives. He is remembered primarily for two important narrative ballads, "Song of Lasting Pain" and "Pipa-Song" (translated also as "The Mandolin Ballad").

In 824, he wrote a farewell to Hangzhou poem as he was about to leave for his next posting as governor of Suzhou. Recently, the city constructed a monumental sculpture beside the lake to evoke the sentiments expressed in this poem, "Good-bye to the People of Hangzhou."

Su Shi of the Song dynasty is the other governor-poet who left his signature on West Lake in the form of a dike that today bears his name, Su causeway. He was the foremost cultural figure in China during the eleventh century. In the 1070s, during his four-year assignment in provincial Hangzhou, he wrote about "always alluring West Lake" with its "Rippling waters shimmering on a sunny day, Misty mountains shrouded in rain." A number of his most frequently reprinted poems date from this period of his life, notably "Billowing Black Clouds: written on the 27th day of the 6th month at the Lake-Watching Tower, drunk."

Before meeting the city in person I tried to prepare myself by reading any information about Hangzhou that I could scrounge from local libraries in Vermont and from interlibrary loan. The sources seemed exotic at the time: depictions of life in the city in either the 1200s from the *Travels of Marco Polo*, or during the late nineteenth and early twentieth centuries as remembered by American children of Christian missionaries. In fact, the Hangzhou that I became acquainted with in 2005 had more in common with the depictions of the earlier period.

French sinologist Jacques Gernet, in his book *Daily Life in China on the Eve of the Mongol Invasion 1250–1276*, expanded upon Marco Polo's description of the city as "the most majestic and wealthy city in the world." He details the "very lively night life ... many districts of the town remained in a state of animation until very late into the night. Multi-coloured lamps lit the entrances and courtyards of restaurants, taverns, and tea-houses, and illumined shop displays" (originally written in French; translated, Macmillan Co., New York, 1962, p. 36). As did Marco Polo, Gernet documents the large population of more than one million inhabitants as well as the vast quantities of rice, pork and salted fish consumed in Hangzhou. He concludes that "several hundred tons of this cereal must have been brought into Hangchow every day, and the rice-barges coming from the great rice-growing regions of Chekiang [i.e., Zhejiang] and of present-day Kiangsu [i.e., Jiangsu] passed unceasingly along its canals. It was a traffic which went on uninterruptedly night and day" (p. 46). Perhaps more surprising is his mention of "a high standard of cleanliness" with "jealous care lavished on maintaining the purity of the lake water," so that "the townspeople, who drink no other water than this [do not] run the risk of epidemics" (p. 45).

The observations from the pens of Americans who had lived in Hangzhou in the late nineteenth and twentieth centuries contrasted on almost every count with the portrait of the city from the thirteenth century. John Leighton Stuart, missionary, president of Yenching University and the last United States ambassador to China before 1949, was born in Hangzhou in 1876 to Southern Presbyterian missionary parents and spent his first eleven years of life there. He wrote in his autobiography that "when my parents settled in Hangchow they found a city much of which had been devastated only a decade before by the ravages of the Taiping Rebellion [1861]. But the beauty of the surrounding country remained, and it made a deep impression on my mother" (*Fifty Years in China: the Memoirs of John Leighton Stuart, Missionary and Ambassador*, NY: Random House, 1954, p.13). Eugenia Barnett Shultheis, an eighty-seven-year-old Californian, had memories of watching the construction of the Christian college rise up alongside the Qiantang River in the south of the city. Her family fled during the summer months to a healthy mountain resort in Mokanshan to avoid "the health hazards of the crowded cities.... The American child of that era in Hangchow could never forget in adulthood that exciting voyage in the Standard Oil Company launch" (*Hangchow, My Home: Growing Up in Heaven Below*, Fort Bragg, CA: Lost Coast Press, 2000, p. 217).

Zhejiang University

As one of China's key universities under the direct administration of the central Ministry of Education, Zhejiang University, or Zheda, as it is commonly called, likes to tout its reputation as the third or fourth most competitive university in the country. Students invariably mention how difficult it was to be admitted, and the faculty vaunts its accomplishments in research, especially in the natural sciences.

The university has a venerable history, founded in 1897 as Qiushi Academy, one of the four oldest western-style institutions of higher learning in China. During its early years, when China was still ruled by the Qing dynasty, the small Confucian academy emphasized the study of science and mathematics and established physics and chemistry laboratories. By 1928 it had grown into a national comprehensive college and was renamed Chekiang (i.e., Zhejiang) University.

In 1952, a few years after the creation of the People's Republic of China, the university was divided into single disciplinary colleges, with Zhejiang retaining the bulk of the science and technology disciplines. At this time a private Christian college called Zhijiang University that had been founded and financed by Americans was closed down and its campus and educational facilities incorporated into other state-run institutions of higher education in Hangzhou. In the late 1950s, Hangzhou University was formed with teaching and research capabilities in both arts and sciences, but not until a 1998 combination of Zhejiang Medical University, Zhejiang Agriculture University, Hangzhou University and the Zhejiang University was the present Zhejiang University established.

The amalgamated university, with more than 40,000 students, two-thirds of whom are undergraduates, and more than 8,000 faculty members, is spread out among six separate campuses. Zijingang, the newest campus, which opened its modern-designed residence halls and teaching buildings only a few years ago, is situated in the marshy northwest suburbs of Hangzhou. This is the location for the School of International Studies, where I taught in the English department.

The two-and-half-room apartment where my husband and I lived was on Yuquan campus, the site of the original Qiushi Academy. Here streets lined with stately sycamore trees stand amidst large banners in red characters announcing the latest academic conferences. Yuquan campus felt more like a village than a university, with grocery stores and hairdressers, a hospital, restaurants, a large outdoor swimming pool, and basketball courts everywhere. The campus is filled with substantial camphors, the designated Hangzhou tree, and osmanthus bushes, the city flower, and includes a small bamboo grove, which was fenced off during sprouting time to discourage poachers of the much-favored bamboo shoots. The most beautiful landscape is the sloping garden with a pond, small bridge, and grassy area behind the library. From here it is a "mere" seven-hundred-step climb to reach the top of the mountain with a panoramic view of the city and West Lake.

Two prominent statues mark the entrance path to the Yuquan campus and provide photo opportunities for students decked out in their graduation tassels and gowns. One is of Mao Zedong, a massive monument erected in 1966 during the Cultural Revolution. Instead of removing it as a relic from the past, as was common practice at other Chinese universities I was told, Zhejiang University has retained its statue of Mao, which remains a popular meeting spot as well as staging ground for morning exercises. Beyond Chairman Mao, and sculpted as a statue in human scale dressed in a western suit, stands Zhu Kezhen, eminent meteorologist and president of the university from 1936 to 1949.

Historical Context

Although Chinese civilization boasts a history of more than 5,000 years, this book covers a much shorter timescale, beginning in most cases with the birth date, October 1, 1949, of the People's Republic of China, or New China, the vernacular name for the country. In two instances, the personal life stories retold here stretch somewhat further back into history to the War of Resistance Against Japanese Aggression, China's name for World War II, which began in 1937 and ended in 1945.

The historical context for this book encompasses four distinct periods in contemporary Chinese history: 1931–1949; 1949–1966; 1966–1976; 1976 to the present. During the first period, under the leadership of Chiang Kai-shek, China was embroiled at first in war with Japan and then in a debilitating civil war. The second period witnessed the birth of the new nation and the launching of a planned society under the direction of Mao Zedong, chairman of the Communist Party of China. The ten years of the Cultural Revolution marked the third era. The last period, in which China is still immersed, is the age of reform, based largely upon the ideas of Deng Xiaoping.

1931–1949

Two grandparents of university students profiled in chapter 1 could remember their lives in the 1930s. One lived in the countryside of occupied north China, in what is today Henan province, and told her granddaughter about being required as a school girl to learn the Japanese language and to worship the emperor of Japan. A student from Shanghai reported that his grandfather had joined up as a soldier after the Lugou Bridge incident on July 7, 1937, and had fought the Japanese as a logistics officer in the Kuomintang (KMT) Army during the eight-year war.

During the 60th anniversary of the end of the war in 2005, the Chinese media were filled with commemorations, screening multipart documentaries on television and continually interviewing veterans and commentators. They ran features on reunions with visiting octogenarian U.S. pilots who had been stationed in Kunming in southwest China, as well as lurid reports of the Nanjing Massacre of December 13, 1937, which resulted in 300,000 Chinese civilian casualties. Japan had invaded China from the northeast and early in the 1930s had established the puppet regime of Manchukuo. Not until mid–1937, when Japan attacked Lugou Bridge near Beijing and then in August mounted a full-scale war on Shanghai, did the Nationalist government enter into a military alliance with the Red Army to counter the Japanese. During the fourteen years of war with Japan, which started on September 18, 1931, and ended on August 15, 1945, China reportedly suffered a loss of 35 million people.

In 2005 Zhejiang University, where I taught, also mounted an exhibit on its wartime history. When Japan began to attack and occupy central and then southern China, the government in Nanjing was forced in November 1937 to move west and to set up a provisional capital in Chongqing that remained there until October 1945. Hangzhou also fell to the Japanese in 1937, and the university, with its laboratories, libraries, professors and students, trekked west on its own 1,000-mile-long march. After several lengthy stops en route to hold classes in borrowed monasteries, schools, and farms, Zhejiang University established a wartime campus in 1938 in Zunyi in Guizhou province. This extremely difficult migration was a compelling testament to the respect of Chinese students and faculty for higher education.

The city of Zunyi, situated approximately 150 miles south of Chongqing, played a pivotal role in twentieth-century China. It was here in January 1935 that Mao Zedong assumed paramount authority of the Communist Party. Zunyi lay at the midway point in the Long March of the Red Army, as it shifted its revolutionary base from southeastern Jianxi province to its wartime headquarters in Yan'an in northwestern Shaanxi province.

Highlighted in Zhejiang University's commemorative display were detailed maps and photographs of buildings and sports teams, and portraits of renowned professors and students. A picture of British sinologist and scientist Joseph Needham, who visited the university in the early 1940s and called Zhejiang University the "Cambridge of the East," was accorded a prominent spot. In May 1946 the university returned to the Yuquan campus in Hangzhou with labs, books and almost three times as many students as had left Hangzhou nine years earlier.

Even after Japan surrendered in August 1945, all was far from well in the land of China. For more than three years civil war raged between the Kuomintang and the Communists, terminating only in 1949 when the Nationalist government of Chiang Kai-shek fled to Taiwan. Two university students reported on their grandmothers' lingering memories of those difficult years, which they both spent in rural regions of north China. In Anhui province, according to Xue Yan's grandmother (see chapter 2), the reputations of the soldiers of the two armies differed; whereas KMT soldiers were cruel to the peasants, "punching men to their heart's content," the soldiers of the Red Army were "lenient and sympathetic to the poor."

In Henan province, Vivian's grandmother (see chapter 1) recollected images of soldiers and cannons cluttering train stations and beggars everywhere amidst soaring prices for food.

1949–1966

In 1949, the so-called never-changing face of China began a transformation that has continued unabated for nearly sixty years. None of the people featured in this book were alive at the founding of New China, but several of their parents and grandparents experienced the heady events of the 1950s.

At the top of the list of changes that were introduced by the new government was the agrarian reform law of June 1950. In rural Funan county, Anhui province, the grandparents of Xue Yan (see chapter 2) were allotted one acre, which, she reports, "absolutely was a blessing for them," because it ended the ever-lingering fear of starvation. Before this land reform her grandmother's family had owned no land of its own, but had served as tenants to rich landlords who took half of their harvests and who had forced her grandmother to work as a spinner when still a child. After the land distribution, her grandmother worked alone in her fields, and sometimes alongside her husband but rarely with her neighbors. The rich landlords departed from her village but she didn't know where they fled.

This 1950 law was the first of a series of policies enacted by the government that changed the ways of life of rural China. In the early 1950s peasants were encouraged to share tools, animals, and even their labor in the setup of mutual-aid cooperatives. Then, with the pooling of their fragmentary plots to create elementary cooperatives, peasants were no longer farming individual landholdings but were contributing investment shares and their labor to a large farm and receiving their incomes from the cooperative. By 1957, when peasants in 96 percent of rural households turned over their land deeds to producers' cooperatives, agricultural villages, run by local councils, selected managers to operate the farms, and villagers were paid wages for work performed.

The ultimate stage in the collectivization of agriculture was the creation of People's Communes, an institution introduced as part of the now discredited Great Leap Forward policy of 1958. According to Mao Zedong's directives the communes were to be big and public and were to feature eating at common dining rooms as well as participating in the construction of public works projects. In only a few months, 740,000 agricultural production cooperatives were merged into 26,000 People's Communes that were centrally managed and organized into production brigades.

Xue Yan's grandmother recalls getting food from "a gigantic iron cauldron and sharing every meal with all the peasants whether aged or young." She also remembers that during "the Great Leap Movement, the Fuyang local government bragged about the harvest and the bounty of its districts and carried out several grand projects, among which digging a gigantic river for irrigation was an important one." As Xue Yan notes, "My grandma carried her first son, my father, to join in this grand project, and she had been laboring far away from her house altogether for three months. Therefore, she did not make steel [out of household pots in backyard furnaces, as was the common endeavor during the Great Leap Forward], but instead dug the river."

History books published in China today describe the Great Leap Forward as a "leftist error," especially the "blind pursuit of productive speed in industry and agriculture" that led to "falsification and embellishment" of yields and grain harvests. By 1960 "the national economy slumped into an extremely difficult situation" (*History and Civilization of China*, Beijing: CIP, 2003, p. 245). Many books that are critical of the policy do not necessarily accord the Great Leap Forward primal responsibility for the extreme food shortages of the winter 1959/60, usually relegating the blame to unusually adverse weather conditions. Three grandparents mentioned the occurrence of famine in their rural areas. In Henan province, Vivian's grandmother (chapter 1) recalled that "there was not enough food and people dug wild plants to eat. Many got diseases and became bloated because of hunger." Anhui province was especially hard hit, a historical fact substantiated by the personal experiences of two of the families in this book. In Fan Gao's family (see chapter 2), his paternal grandfather died from starvation in 1959, and Xue Yan (see chapter 2) reported that "The 1959 wide-scale famine was ingrained in my grandma's mind, and it was a horrible nightmare for her, for one of her children didn't survive that famine."

In the 1950s it was actually not agriculture but heavy industry that garnered most of the government's attention. After a three-year period of rehabilitation and recovery of the economy that lasted from 1949 to 1952 and included two years and nine months (October 1950 to July 1953) spent fighting the Korean War, New China launched its first Five Year Plan. Modeled after state economic planning in the Soviet Union, the policies prioritized the development of heavy industry. The industrial revolution was skewed toward steel-rolling, coal-mining, and oil-drilling in the three provinces of northeast China, where the Japanese had established their wartime enterprises. Under the first Five Year Plan, the government began its public ownership of production with the establishment of state-owned companies that provided not only employment but also housing, schools, medical care, and social security — what Chinese refer to as the "iron rice bowl."

Beyond developments in northeast China, the new Chinese government invested in capital construction projects at the average rate of one new one starting up every three days. One of these, the site where Shirley's parents met (see chapter 4), was the Xin'an River Hydropower station in Zhejiang province. Thousand Island Lake, now a prime tourist destination, was created as a byproduct of this massive construction project that was completed in 1959.

In the first decade after the founding of the People's Republic of China international relations were based on a policy of "Leaning to One Side," skewed towards the socialist countries and in particular the Soviet Union. Not only did the alliance with the Soviet Union impact economic, political and military policies, but Soviet models influenced Chinese educational policy as well. Even in the 1960s, after China and the Soviet Union's abrupt parting and estrangement, An Xin's mother (see chapter 3) did not have the opportunity in school to learn English, which had been eliminated from the curriculum in the early 1950s. Instead, she studied the Russian language, and many foreign language departments in Chinese schools and universities retained a surfeit of Russian teachers well into the 1980s.

Not all international contacts in the 1950s were with socialist countries, for Premier Zhou Enlai in a speech before twenty-nine Asian and African countries at the Bandung Conference in Indonesia in 1955 spelled out what has remained the basic principle of Chinese foreign policy. "The Chinese delegation has come for the purpose of seeking unity, not to pick quarrels. There is no need to trumpet one's ideology, or the differences that exist among us. We are here to seek a community of views, not to raise points of difference" (quoted in Han Suyin, *Eldest Son*, NY: Hill and Wang, 1994, p. 245). In 2006 China's President Hu Jintao reiterated the same sentiment at Yale University: "Differences in ideology, social system and development model should not stand in the way of exchanges among civilizations; still less should they become excuses for mutual confrontation. We should uphold the diversity of the world, enhance dialogue and interaction between civilizations, and draw on each other's strength instead of practicing mutual exclusion."

Not only did the policies enacted by New China transform economics, politics, and foreign relations, but the lives of Chinese women also changed fundamentally. As Vivian's grandmother in chapter 1 reported, "After Liberation, the new government encouraged women to work and I also began to work." She was employed at a factory in Zhengzhou, a newly industrializing city in central China, while Evelyn's grandmother (see chapter 1) went to work at a silk factory in Hangzhou where she learned to read. Paid maternity leaves for 56 days were instituted for working mothers, and the marriage law of 1950 guaranteed free choice of partner, monogamy, and equal rights for both sexes.

At the beginning of the 1960s, China devoted several years to recovery and readjustment as the country retrenched from changes carried out too hurriedly and reacted to being left on its own resources after the termination of the alliance with the Soviet Union. Targets planned for completion in the course of the Second Five Year Plan were not achieved until 1965, although in October 1964 China touted a military technological advance: explosion of its first atomic bomb.

First and foremost, after the devastating famine of the "three bitter years," from 1959 to 1962, food production was given top priority. Industry was geared to assist agriculture, as steel parts went to manufacture agricultural equipment and factories were built to boost the supply of chemical fertilizers. After the Sino-Soviet split, the government decided to disperse industry away from established centers in northeast China and along the east coast. The "third front policy" emphasized the industrialization of remote inland areas, far away from international borders. Gansu province in northwest China was a new focal region, the childhood home of Professor Xue-Qun Chen (see chapter 5) and also where today's leaders (Hu Jintao and Wen Jiabao) first went to work after graduating from universities in Beijing.

1966–1976

In May 1966 the Central Committee of the Communist Party of China adopted a decision concerning the Great Proletarian Cultural Revolution, launching what the government today refers to as "a catastrophic decade for the Chinese nation." For ten years the country was embroiled in domestic turmoil marked by big character posters, destruction of traditional cultural landmarks, infighting among political cadres, abuse and violence perpetrated against intellectuals, and mass rallies of Red Guards shouting Mao quotations from the *Little Red Book*. Many books have been written by Chinese who were targets of the Cultural Revolution, and academics in economics, politics, education, and the arts have decried and documented damages inflicted upon Chinese society.

After hearing from other Chinese people about their experiences during the Cultural Revolution and especially after reading *The Unknown Cultural Revolution* (2000) by Dongping Han, I have realized that this assessment may not take into consideration all aspects of the history of those years. Not everything that occurred during that tumultuous period impacted Chinese society in a totally negative manner. The thirteen real-life stories in this book present contrasting versions of this historical era. Human reactions and interactions in response to economic hardship and injustice led in some cases to a strengthening of character with positive impact on future lives.

My students invariably commented in their essays about parents who, unlike themselves, never enjoyed the opportunity to receive a college education. I learned from reading more than one hundred essays that the national college entrance examinations were canceled from 1966 to 1976. During those years only children of workers and peasants were admitted to universities without taking a competitive examination. Many students also wrote about the wasted years when their parents had been forced to do manual labor in the countryside.

Out of all my students, William (see chapter 1) was the only one who could relate personal stories of persecution in his family. His parents, but in particular his mother, who was born in 1955, could never achieve as much in life as her own parents, William believed, because of the Cultural Revolution. When his mother finished school in the early 1970s, she was sent to the countryside on Chongming island at the mouth of the Yangtze

19

River, across from the port of Shanghai. She never received higher education and was therefore deprived of professional employment. In contrast, her parents were both professionals and enjoyed long and satisfying careers.

William's grandparents, who were both employed in Shanghai when the Cultural Revolution struck, suffered from abuses during this era but in fact remained unharmed. His grandmother, who had graduated from teacher's college in the 1940s, taught school in Shanghai for many years. He wrote:

> In 1967, being an excellent teacher with a family milieu of landlord, which was equated to intimacy with feudalism, my grandma was gradually degraded into an ordinary cleaner assigned with laborious and meaningless dustings and moppings.... Around 1977, she was rehabilitated from the oppressed status and taught until the mid–1980s.
>
> My grandpa, who was an officer in a regiment of the KMT Army, was placed in a financial organization in Shanghai after the victory in 1945. Many of his colleagues chose to flee to Taiwan with the KMT, and he was thus invited. But he remained in Shanghai.... In 1967 periodically, a bunch of Red Guard soldiers would break into my grandpa's house searching for ironclad evidence for prosecuting while at the same time sneaking something or smashing something at will. My mother can still vaguely remember how it happened. "Bunches of people rushed in, hailing Long Live Chairman Mao! Down with Feudalism! Down with Authority! and all kinds of slogans. They smashed vases and were quite rude to everyone in the house." My grandpa couldn't escape from the heavy laborious job, either. He retired in 1977 and died of lung cancer at the age of 76 in 1990.

In contrast to the fate of William's family during the Cultural Revolution, Evelyn's father (see chapter 1) reported that the two years he spent doing farm work in the countryside near Hangzhou in the mid–1970s "helped him a lot in his future life and in particular developed his strong will." Others, who were part of the generation of urban teenagers mobilized by the government to go "up to the mountains and down to the villages" to learn values and skills from tough, self-sufficient peasants, also commented on the benefits that accrued from that experience. An English professor who spent three years in the countryside in Zhejiang province doing "all sorts of work" told me that he believed "young people today are spoiled. That's because they have never endured hardship nor have they acquired the strength of character learned from overcoming difficulties."

Other Chinese recall the primitive living conditions prevalent during the Cultural Revolution. A movie buff has described watching films "free of charge, on open ground, projected on to a piece of white cloth attached to two poles. Electricity for the projector came from a generator activated by someone pedaling a bicycle" ("Living with Films" by Yu Xiangjun, *China Today*, September 2005, p. 22). An eminent English professor who grew up in Hangzhou told me that the only time he ever swam in West Lake was during the Cultural Revolution. "There were no rules then," he said.

One iconoclastic Chinese academic, Dongping Han, who grew up in a rural village in Shandong province during the Cultural Revolution, is not equivocal about his positive depiction of that decade. He contends "that the political convulsions of the Cultural Revolution democratized village political culture and spurred the growth of rural education" (Dongping Han, *The Unknown Cultural Revolution: Educational Reforms and Their Impact on China's Rural Development*, NY: Garland Publishing, 2000, p.1). In his book, written as a doctoral dissertation for Brandeis University, he refutes the Chinese government's assessment and a view that has been "widely endorsed by Chinese intellectuals and echoed by Western academics ... that the Cultural Revolution trampled individual rights, devastated the education system and led to economic catastrophe" (p. 1).

Han's argument rests on data collected in his hometown in Jimo County, situated near the port city of Qingdao. He credits the educational reforms of the Cultural Revolution with leading to the "empowerment of the rural people" (p. 116). Instead of criticizing workers' and farmers' participation in the management of schools and the integrating of academic education with productive labor, he stresses that these policies helped to spread education among the village population. At the same time, he points to a growth in the number of rural primary and junior middle schools that made it possible for children to attend school without traveling great distances. As for high school education during the Cultural Revolution, he emphasizes that in Jimo County the expansion from two high schools in 1965 to eighty-four in 1976, "all of which were constructed and financed by communes" (p. 103), enabled "about 70 percent of school-age children in the commune to attend these high schools free of charge and without passing any screening tests" (p. ix).

Having read Dongping Han's book about what he asserts were the positive effects of the Cultural Revolution on educating children in rural China, I wondered how Zhejiang University had weathered the storm of those years. I interviewed a retired mathematics professor, Guan Zhicheng, who had entered the university as a student in 1955. According to Professor Guan, turmoil at the university lasted for only two years, from 1966 to 1968, but no new students were admitted into the mathematics department until 1973. Before the reinstatement of national college entrance examinations in 1977, students were selected for admission to university from personal recommendations, and workers and peasants were favored. Even though most students who were accepted between 1973 and 1977 had received only limited academic preparation in middle schools and were on the whole "very poor students," he recalled that there had been a few "who were clever" and who had stayed on to become university professors.

Professor Guan also remembered attending big meetings where individuals were publicly criticized. He, as a junior professor, did not suffer personally but was reassigned away from the university to apply his knowledge of mathematics for nonacademic purposes. For one year he worked at the Shanghai shipyard as a weather forecaster and then he was sent to a hydroelectric power station to calculate potential operational dangers.

While China was still embroiled in the Cultural Revolution, a transformation in China's foreign relations occurred during 1971 and 1972. China welcomed a ping pong team from the United States in April 1971 and President Nixon's National Security adviser, Henry Kissinger, in July 1971. In October 1971, the People's Republic of China replaced the Republic of China on the Security Council at the United Nations, and in February 1972 President Nixon shook hands with Mao Zedong in Beijing, overturning more than twenty years of frigid relations between the USA and New China. This warming up led to burgeoning enthusiasm for studying English, reflected in Ian's personal story (see chapter 5).

1976 to the present

Mao Zedong died in September 1976, the same year that saw the demise of Premier Zhou Enlai in January. Hua Guo-feng, who had been designated by Chairman Mao as his successor, assumed paramount leadership of the country after Mao's death and immediately arrested the Gang of Four (Wang Hong-wen, Zhang Chun-qiao, Jiang Qing [Mao's wife], and Yao Wen-yuan), who had plotted to "usurp state power" and had committed "heinous crimes" during the Cultural Revolution (*Peking Review*, October 29, 1976).

The chairmanship of Hua Guo-feng lasted for only two years, until 1978, when Deng Xiaoping effectively took over the leadership of New China. He advocated what were to become familiar trademarks of his rule: pragmatism, political acumen and strength, and an uncanny ability to promote economic policies that benefited the majority of the Chinese people. China flourished during the era of Deng Xiaoping, and in 2005 Chinese society still appeared to be immersed in that period of history.

Two new leaders, both of whom he selected, have succeeded him. Jiang Zemin assumed the post of general secretary of the Communist Party in June 1989, became president in 1993, and, upon the death of Deng Xiaoping at the age of 92 in 1997, was designated paramount leader of the People's Republic of China. In March 2003 he officially stepped down and passed on the leadership to Hu Jintao.

Officially, what Deng Xiaoping started in 1978 is called reform of the economy and opening up to the world. He said that the country was building socialism with Chinese characteristics, moving away from a centrally planned economy towards a market orientation. The government's five-year plans guided the economic expansion, and government funding steered the growth in designated directions. There were ups and downs and readjustments. In particular, during the economic slowdown from 1988 to 1991 the government curtailed market-inspired structural reforms, and at the end of the 1990s and into the beginning of the twenty-first century, when grain harvests fell precipitously, the government reasserted macroeconomic adjustments to stimulate agricultural production. Today, the government speaks about deepening reform, creating common prosperity and a harmonious society, but does not talk of returning to policies of the past. At the same time, while encouraging economic reform China has been hesitant to undertake broad political reform. The Communist Party of China (CCP) has maintained one-party political control as was made blatantly clear in 1989, when the military put down pro-democracy student protests in Tian'anmen Square.

During my year in China, the concept of competition was the "Thought of Deng Xiaoping" most frequently quoted: "In economic policy, I think we should allow some regions and enterprises and some workers and peasants to earn more and enjoy more benefits sooner than others, in accordance with their hard work and greater contributions to society. If the standard of living of some people is raised first, this will inevitably be an impressive example to their neighbors, and people in other regions and units will want to learn from them. This will help the whole national economy to advance wave upon wave" ("Emancipate the Mind, Seek Truth from Facts and Unite as One in Looking to the Future," Speech to China Communist Party, December 13, 1978).

The university students, whose life stories make up the largest portion of *Students and Teachers of the New China*, have spent their twenty-some years in this era. They never knew life under Chairman Mao, who is regarded today as New China's founding father. They never experienced the "iron rice-bowl system that refers to a job that is stable and guaranteed for life, just like a real iron bowl that will never be broken." According to Li Haibo, editor in chief of *Beijing Review*, some people in China today are expressing nostalgia for that system as the society grows more polarized and income gaps widen (Li Haibo, "Will Egalitarianism Return?" in *Beijing Review*, March 31, 2005, p. 48).

Only when comparing the life experiences of those born in the 1980s with those of their parents, who were born in the 1950s, can one appreciate the vastness of the changes undertaken during the era of Deng Xiaoping. Everything from standard of living, to job opportunities, to familial relations, to culture and entertainment has been transformed. Students' parents remember food rationing and the first time they watched television; their children remember their first cell phone and are accustomed to listening to music and to viewing movies from the Internet. Washing machines and refrigerators, commonplace household items today, were relatively unknown in the 1960s and 1970s. Chinese people born in the 1950s grew up with many siblings, whereas their own children are the only child in the family. For employment, the common practice was either for the government to make the assignment or to inherit the job from a parent. Now young people compete in the marketplace to find their jobs. Perhaps the most significant difference between parents and children are their values in life. The generation of the 1950s was raised with communism's

24

selfless ideals, whereas young adults today search for their beliefs amidst a vast range of choices.

The period from 1976 to the present may appear to be easier to comprehend because it is contemporary and the language used to describe change may sound more familiar. Yet, there are interpretations of policies and reactions that are particularly Chinese. I have enumerated in the following paragraphs some of the more crucial reforms initiated by Deng Xiaoping, in agriculture, industry, education, and international relations, in an attempt to provide a foundation for understanding the changing lives of the Chinese people presented in this book.

In agriculture, farm production and rural life were reformed, with the introduction of the household responsibility system in 1982 that linked individual household income to farm output. Rural land continued to be collectively owned, but farmers were allocated plots of land that held 30-year leases. This reform policy dissolved the community support system that had provided for health care, education, and social security. In industry, starting in 1979 Special Economic Zones were established in four coastal cities to operate as centers for foreign investment and export production, and in 1984 fourteen more coastal cities were added to the list. Chinese people migrated in droves to labor in coastal factories or to build the infrastructure for these cities. Local governmental industries, called township and village enterprises, sprouted up in rural areas, producing consumer goods and in some cases competing with state-owned enterprises for funds, raw materials and markets.

In education, there was at first a return to the system that had been established before the Cultural Revolution. Examinations were reinstituted as were academic titles, and "once again the initiative of educational workers for achievement and the enthusiasm of students for study were brought into play" (China Handbook Series, *Education and Science* by China Handbook Editorial Committee, Beijing, 1983, p. 24). Nine years of schooling were made compulsory.

Deng Xiaoping's reforms changed the way that schools in China are administered and financed. Local governments, instead of the central government, were given the responsibility to manage education, and they began charging tuition and miscellaneous fees for attendance at elementary and middle schools. The reforms of the 1980s thus made the achievement of universal compulsory schooling in China an impossible goal.

Many rural parents, even with their increased incomes that resulted from Deng Xiaoping's agricultural reforms, could not afford to pay for their children's education.

Among the wide array of reforms there was one, the family planning law of 1979, which coupled onto all the others. Not only did the policy of encouraging each Chinese family to give birth to only one child reduce total population growth by more than 300 million, it also made it possible to spread the benefits accruing from a booming economy to a larger proportion of the population. University students who were born in the 1980s came from one-child families by and large, whereas their parents grew up as one of many siblings.

In the realm of international relations, Deng Xiaoping is renowned for initiating the policy of "One Country, Two Systems" that allowed for the peaceful restoration of Chinese sovereignty over Hong Kong in 1997 and Macao in 1999. During my year in China, history was made when the leader of the Kuomintang Party on Taiwan, Lien Chan, stepped onto Chinese soil for the first time since the founding of the People's Republic of China in 1949 and met with President Hu Jintao.

Not only were diplomatic policies changed but also China's military and security expenditures were reduced sharply in the 1980s under Deng Xiaoping's reforms. "When the country became preoccupied with reviving the economy ... negative growth in defense spending was witnessed for seven years in a row," Peng Guangqian of the Chinese Academy of Military Science reported in *China Daily* on March 15, 2006.

Since the 1990s, however, the defense budget has steadily grown. In 2007 China announced a 17.8 percent increase from the previous year to reach $44.94 billion. Yet, with less than 8 percent of the government's annual spending directed toward the military, China devotes a smaller proportion of its budget to ensuring its defense needs than most other countries. In comparison, the president of the United States requested $439.3 billion for the Department of Defense's 2007 base budget with hefty supplements for war funding. President Hu Jintao continues to preach "peace and development," emphasizing the negative impact of military confrontation to China's future. At Yale University in April 2006, Hu said: "China holds high the banner of peace, development and cooperation. It pursues an independent foreign policy of peace and commits itself firmly to peaceful development."

Students and Teachers of the New China is divided into three sections, presenting real-life stories of students, teachers, and children "who are the faces of the future." The book focuses on thirteen Chinese who were born between the 1950s and the beginning of the twenty-first century. All lived in Hangzhou in 2005 although many were temporary dwellers there, in most cases residing at Zhejiang University while studying.

The three chapters that comprise the first part of the book describe the lives of eight university students who were born between 1981 and 1985. Half grew up in northern China and half in the south, demarcated by the Yangtze River. Five of the students came from urban areas and three from rural areas.

Part two, consisting of two chapters, spotlights five teachers, four of whom are native to Zhejiang province. The chapter entitled "Born in the 1970s" portrays three teachers of English who are employed at various levels of educational institutions. The other chapter in this section, "Born in the 1960s and 1950s," features two professors at Zhejiang University, one in the science faculty and one in the School of International Studies.

The third part of the book looks toward the future. The chapter called "Born in the 1990s" focuses on the lives of children who are growing up in China today, and it includes descriptions of visits to specific primary and middle schools. In the concluding chapter, I discuss some of the hurdles as well as some of the ideas being professed in China as it strives to create a moderately prosperous, harmonious society.

PART ONE: STUDENTS

As a professor of English at Zhejiang University I found no dearth of Chinese students to interview. Initially I invited my English-major students, who were disproportionately women, to participate in my project, subject to their parents' agreeing to the publication of their personal stories. With more than 100 students in my four classes, I thought that this would yield a large pool of potential interviewees, especially with the addition of parents and grandparents. Several students, however, who were eager to participate had to drop out because their parents refused to assent, but I ended up with six volunteer undergraduates: five juniors from the advanced English writing course and one sophomore from the English short-fictions course. They were four females and two males, born between 1982 and 1985, four of whom came from cities and two from rural villages. Not a bad beginning.

Then I met An Xin and Xue Yan, both graduate students in English literature and both assigned to me as teaching assistants, one semester after the other. Each already had graduated from university as majors in English and had come to Zhejiang University to study for a master's degree. An Xin received her bachelor's degree from Xi'an International Studies University and Xue Yan from the principal university of Anhui province in Hefei. Because Hangzhou was a not a familiar place to either of them, my husband and I explored the city and environs with each of them. With no exaggeration, each young woman became not only a friend but a part of our family.

29

What happened with these eight subjects was much more revealing than I expected. Not only did I interview each one several times and was able to meet several of their parents, but I also traveled with them, heard about their loves, dreams, depressions, concerns about finding a good job and read a few of their superlative poems and essays, all written in English.

These university students were all born at the beginning of China's opening up era after 1978. They never experienced the governmental policies of Chairman Mao and were not alive during the Cultural Revolution. None of their parents had attended university, for higher education during the Cultural Revolution (1966–1976), which was the very decade when their parents finished school, had been cut back drastically. Many universities held no classes, and those that did admitted students without requiring them to take the National College Entrance Examination.

Undergraduates at Zhejiang University today all had excelled at their previous schools, for this university is ranked highly in academic performance in China. Studying at Zhejiang is roughly the equivalent of being

An Xin, Madelyn Holmes, Xue Yan, Lewis Holmes at Zhejiang University, Zijingang campus.

accepted at Harvard, Yale or Princeton. All had studied English for at least eight years, beginning in junior middle school, and the majority had attended government-supported boarding schools during their final three years of schooling.

They all expressed anxieties about their future lives, for in China the planned economy has been replaced by a more open economic environment and that affects university students directly. Before and until the late 1990s, university authorities would inform graduating seniors of their job assignments. English majors were placed as teachers, usually in colleges or other institutes of higher education, or else in administrative jobs at government offices or businesses. During the past six years, with the change of policy, students have been left to fend for themselves. Most have gravitated to civil service exams, hoping to find a secure government position that pays well, and many have opted to continue postgraduate studies. Pressures have increased to interview with companies, both domestic and foreign, and the worries about what to do next have come to dominate students' final year at university.

Recently, university graduates have been encouraged to start up their own businesses. The focus of most start-ups by people in their twenties is in the Internet sector, and young entrepreneurs are able to benefit from venture capital funds that have become more accessible than they were during the 1990s. At least one of the students in this book started up a company upon graduation from Zhejiang University. Fan Gao and a friend launched an English and Chinese translation service, which during its first year translated more than one million words.

The Chinese government also has initiated a service-oriented alternative for graduates who are willing to look beyond the ultra-competitive job market on the eastern seaboard. Called "Serving the West Project," the program has similarities to AmeriCorps. For those with a spirit of adventure as well as a large dose of old-fashioned communist idealism, there are teaching and community service jobs in the Chinese hinterland available for one-tenth the salary they would receive in cities.

University students all resided in dormitories at Zijingang campus, which is the newest addition to Zhejiang University. The undergraduates shared with seven classmates one large bedroom/study that was furnished with individual single beds, desks and cupboards, and with clotheslines outside for drying laundry, whereas the graduate students shared the same-sized room with only three classmates. Opened in fall 2002, this campus, which is located in the northwestern edge of Hangzhou, is an ambitious attempt by the city to construct twenty-first century-designed buildings and landscaping in a formerly swampy, marginal farming area. However, it is a new campus, which means that the trees are only as tall as an adult male, and walking at a brisk pace from the dormitories to the classrooms takes at least twenty minutes. All the students ride bicycles, but Fan Gao frankly admitted that he had cried when he arrived at Zijingang—"it looked so desolate."

The first part of the book consists of three chapters, separated into urban and rural students. Five of the eight undergraduate and graduate students whom I interviewed were urban Chinese, and three were born and raised in the countryside. Chapter 1 features Evelyn and William, who grew up in the southern Chinese cities of Hangzhou and Shanghai, as well as Sunnie and Vivian, who came from the northern cities of Beijing and Zhengzhou. Chapter 2 shifts to rural students: Wendy, who grew up in Hunan province; and Fan Gao and Xue Yan, who were born and raised in Anhui province, the neighbor province to Zhejiang. Chapter 3 focuses on only one student, An Xin, whose family resides in the small northern city of Xianyang, which abuts Xi'an, the capital of Shaanxi province.

1

Urban Undergraduates Born in the 1980s

China's cities, especially on the east coast, are the most prosperous regions of the country. When statistics compare per capita incomes between urban and rural areas, the city dwellers come out far ahead, so much so that it has become common in China to worry about the income gap between rich and poor. During my year in Hangzhou, I often was made aware of another divide, that between north and south. These differences were not solely economic, and I was not always clear whether they were as important as some Chinese thought them to be. However, I have divided my urban students into northerners and southerners. Evelyn and William come from southern China; Sunnie and Vivian come from the north.

Evelyn

Of all my students Evelyn most closely resembled her place of origin and was most tightly bound to her home and family. She is a pretty girl of medium height, graceful in speech and movement, and at home in Hangzhou, where her family has resided for generations. She is the first member of her family to attend university, and her parents, who both work as civil servants for the municipal government, are proud of her academic achievements. Her career aspirations are tied to Hangzhou, as well, for she wants to find an administrative job in the education department of the city or province.

Childhood

Evelyn, an only child, was born on August 15, 1984, to working-class parents who had married a year earlier. Her parents had met each other several years before, while they both were doing their stint in the countryside outside Hangzhou. During the 1970s, when her parents completed their schooling, it was common policy for Chinese teenagers to spend two years working on farms, and it was not uncommon for romances to spring up during this period away from home. Although their standard of living was still at a meager level in 1983, Evelyn's parents celebrated their wedding with a party at the groom's house and enjoyed a three-day honeymoon to the seaside at Putuo, an island off the coast of Zhejiang province. Her mother remembers buying food with coupons and washing clothes by hand, but also receiving their first television set as a wedding present.

When Evelyn was born, her father, who was twenty-six, was employed as a driving instructor for the Hangzhou transportation department. Her mother, who was twenty-four, took 56 days maternity leave from the spinning division of the silk factory where she worked.

It was Evelyn's maternal grandmother who took care of the baby. She had retired from her own job as a worker at the same silk factory in order to carry Evelyn to be breast fed by her mother in the factory. I learned later that this division of infant care between mother and grandmother was not the normal arrangement in China. It has been a longstanding tradition for the father's family to shoulder this responsibility, and if the father's parents were unable to assist then a more distant relative on the father's side would be called in.

Evelyn maintained an unusually warm relationship with her grandparents, because as a child she lived in their Hangzhou apartment in a close-knit downtown neighborhood. Her grandmother, who was born in 1934 and worked at the silk factory for more than thirty years, never attended school but learned to read while working at the factory. Evelyn's

Evelyn with her parents.

paternal grandmother, who was nearly the same age, had been employed in the cafeteria at the same Hangzhou silk factory and had remained illiterate. Both grandfathers, who had been born in the late 1920s, had received some elementary schooling. Her maternal grandfather had worked at the Hangzhou glass factory and had retired at the age of sixty in 1985, and her paternal grandfather had worked at a textile dyeing plant.

Education

Evelyn began her schooling in 1990 at the same neighborhood school that her mother had attended in the late 1960s. The school grounds were large, even though they were situated in the midst of old apartment buildings, and there was a sizeable playground. When I visited this four-story primary school with Evelyn and her mother, a first-grade class was practicing writing Chinese characters, and many parents seated on very low chairs were giving their children a helping hand.

Her memories of primary school are filled with singing revolutionary songs, boys and girls playing together, and elderly women teachers who were very warm to the children. Corporal punishment was against the law and naughty children were assigned to copy and recopy Chinese characters. She recalls that one teacher left her classroom when she became enraged at the children's bad behavior.

As a child Evelyn was always reading books and liked fairy tales in particular, but she did not like sports. "I ran very slowly," she confesses, and "I was very shy in school." But by grade 3 she had become a class monitor and, as she puts it, "my life was colorful." As monitor, she led the singing of the national anthem at the weekly school assemblies and participated actively in cleaning the classrooms and standing at the front gate to welcome visitors.

After six years at the community school, she started commuting by bus to a key middle school in another section of the city, where she "was always working hard." She liked Chinese and math, but found chemistry and physics difficult. At this school "we concentrated on passing tests," a description that I often heard about Chinese junior middle schools. She also started studying English at this school, and the curriculum included politics and some history lessons as well. She remembers liking her math teacher especially, "probably because she was my mother's friend, and she took care of me."

By the end of her three years at this school, Evelyn decided that she wanted to attend a key high school in a distant region of Hangzhou, where she would need to board. She passed the entrance exam for this government-supported school, and now at age fifteen felt that she was ready to make her own decisions without the constant guidance of her parents. But as she explained to me, it was more shocking than she had expected, and she soon became so ill that she had to return home for a while. But she persevered and managed to get along with the eight girls in her dormitory room and to eat the institutional food. She admitted that she looked forward to the weekly gifts of delicious food that her father brought. In her family, father was the cook, a skill he had acquired while in the countryside, and he told me through Evelyn's interpretation that he especially enjoyed cooking fish. Her mother never learned to cook.

Even though moving to this school in 1999 proved to be a major transition in her life, and she continued to phone her parents every day, nevertheless the friends she made during these three years were her most enduring ones. Academically, she did not change, continuing to enjoy math, Chinese, and history and rejecting science, especially chemistry. She read the Brontë sisters' novels in Chinese, embraced the world of computers and cultivated a new-found interest in films: "*Titanic* was the first movie I saw, and I still enjoy watching Disney cartoons." In fact, her first aspiration was to become a filmmaker, but instead she chose to pursue a university education after doing well on the college-entrance examination. Economics was her first choice of major, but she accepted her second choice, English, with a specialty in literature.

Parents

Evelyn's parents are in their late forties, and their childhoods, education, and working lives have differed enormously from their daughter's. Yet they, too, have experienced a changing China, and their personal lives have changed along with their country.

Evelyn's father, who was born in 1958 in Hangzhou, grew up in a family with three brothers, all of whom are still living in this city. After completing nine years of schooling and working for two years in the countryside, he joined the army. He served for three years in western Sichuan province, where he learned to drive before returning to Hangzhou to find employment as a driver of buses and trucks for the provincial transportation department. Assisted by a strong will, he has been able to move up in the career ladder, working as a driving instructor and now as manager of the bus and car division in the police department.

His standard of living has continued to improve, from the time in the early 1980s when he built his own house. He had renovated this in the late 1990s and now was moving the family into a newly constructed downtown apartment. A few years ago he purchased a Chinese-made automobile (Xia Li) and was able to pay for it (70,000 *yuan* or $9,000) in cash.

Traveling has been another indication of his increased level of prosperity. His family has been able to take holidays around China, beginning with one to the southern city of Shenzhen in 1987. They travel with tourist groups and have been to Beijing, Dalian, and Qingdao, and they are planning an upcoming trip to Hong Kong. During the summer of 2005, Evelyn's parents paid for her university-sponsored trip to Los Angeles.

Her mother, who was born in 1960, grew up in a large Hangzhou family of three children. She completed nine years of schooling, spent two years in the countryside, and went to work in 1979 at the same silk factory as her mother. By 1994 she was able to leave this factory and to try out a variety of other types of jobs that included spending months at home as a full-time housewife and mother. When Evelyn entered Zhejiang University in 2002, her mother began an administrative job in the bicycle division of the police department, where her father also is employed. She will retire at age fifty and her husband at age sixty, the stipulated retirement ages respectively for women and men.

University of California, Los Angeles (UCLA)

On the last day of spring semester, Evelyn came up to me after class to reveal her exciting news: she had been selected as one of sixteen undergraduates to take part in a five-week summer exchange program with the University of California, Los Angeles. When she later returned to Hangzhou, she told me that "yes, she had had a wonderful experience," and her first wish was to take her parents to visit Los Angeles in the future.

"What had she liked about her trip?" I questioned. She answered: the buildings at UCLA, which "looked like a real university"; the "very energetic" English teachers; the "very comfortable" dorm room; the buildings and setting of the Getty Museum; fire trucks arriving five minutes after the fire alarm sounded; Disneyland; seeing a live television show. In fact, she did not find much to complain about, except for the cold breakfasts, raw vegetables, and the taxi driver who couldn't find their dormitory when they first arrived in Los Angeles: "He let us off on the campus, but after our long flight from China we had to walk around with our luggage for twenty minutes until we located our dormitory."

What did she think of the Americans she met? "We didn't meet very many, because the university students were away for the summer, but people whom we met on the street or bus thought that I was a Mexican because of my dark skin." Evelyn surprised me with this comment, because I had never noticed her particularly dark skin. She expressed amazement about American perceptions of China: "Americans didn't know anything about China as it is today. They thought we were still revolutionaries."

Even though Evelyn likes American culture and was able to enjoy the cultural offerings of Los Angeles, she found several aspects perplexing. Appreciating the art at the Getty Museum was difficult, "because we don't know much about Western painting and sculpture." She was astonished by the audience at a jazz concert: "There were only older people in attendance, whereas in China young people really like jazz." She was unprepared for the racial diversity of the city. "We often rode on public buses, and in Los Angeles only black people took them. That was a surprise, but they were friendly to us," she added.

William

In 2005 William was a sophomore at Zhejiang University. He also had grown up in a southern Chinese city, namely Shanghai, but that is the only feature he has in common with Evelyn. Emotionally, he has already left his family behind as he explores and exploits not only the university's intellectual and cultural opportunities but also the potential resources of every foreign professor who comes to teach at Zhejiang University. I first met William when he took my English short-fictions class, but I had already seen him in the faculty office that we foreign experts shared. He was friends with Judy, the elderly American who taught English the year before I arrived; and he also had befriended Ann, the young American teacher from Iowa, and Margherita, the young Italian teacher.

My personal friendship with William dates from the week-long, October National Day holiday, when my husband and I arranged to meet William in Shanghai and to spend two days experiencing the city with him as our guide. He showed us tourist sites, from the traditional YuYuan garden to XinTiandi, the latest restaurant and entertainment district; he took us to key high school number 4, the one he had attended from 2001 to 2004, to his favorite local restaurants that both he and his mother had frequented, and accompanied us to a Shaoxing opera performance, where he simultaneously interpreted plot and song lyrics.

Childhood

William was born on October 21, 1985, in Shanghai and spent his early years living with his parents on nearby Chongming island. Now being developed in part as an urban center and in part as parkland and a recreational area for the burgeoning 18 million Shanghainese, the island remained a rural backwater outside of the city's cultural reach until very recently. The only images William could recall of his childhood home were negative ones, conditioned by what his parents have chosen to remember, for his childhood cannot be divorced from his family's background. His parents, who were thirty and thirty-one when their only child was born, had lived on Chongming island since the days of the Cultural Revolution when the island was used for reeducation of accused citizens. William's maternal grandparents had upper-class origins and his mother's father had been an officer in the KMT Army. William's mother and her three brothers had not thrived in Mao's China and were discriminated against during the Cultural Revolution.

In the early 1990s William and his parents moved to the Yang Pu district of northeast Shanghai, where William attended primary and junior middle school. His mother worked as an accountant and then transferred to the sales department of a factory producing machine tools. His father's familial origins are unknown to William, but he does know that his paternal grandparents died when his father and his two older sisters were children. His father worked at first as an engineer and then spent ten years driving a taxi.

Education

When William was admitted to Jianping Senior High School, Shanghai's number four key high school, in the fall of 2001, his childhood vanished forever. The sixteen-year-old young man boarded at the school and began his ascent into the world of books and culture. He started reading and has never paused; he fell in love and wrote an unpublished novel about his love affair; he became fluent in English; and he was influenced by a teacher "who wanted to plant Chinese ideas in our souls and make the ideas take root in us."

Jianping is a high school with a strong sense of its own history and a special mission in the realm of education. As a visitor enters the campus, which is located in Shanghai's throbbing, financial district of Pudong, the school motto offers an initial greeting: "Today I am proud of Jianping, tomorrow Jianping will be proud of me." While I took a photograph of William at the entrance standing in front of a large sculpture of a golden apple, he explained that a new principal had already added his personal signature to Jianping since William's graduation only one and half years ago. Now the school motto has been embellished with four new words: openness, democracy, harmony, progressivism.

When William was a Jianping student, there was overwhelming emphasis on academic achievement and on future success. Each of the 1,000 students in his class had a computer at his or her classroom desk, and the class was divided into three levels for instruction: A, B, and C. Students chose to concentrate in humanities or sciences. William chose science at first but later changed to humanities, which meant that he studied history, foreign languages, Chinese literature, economics, politics, music, art, but also some physics, math, and chemistry. At the entrance to the classroom building, a grand piano that had been donated by an alumnus welcomed us, and the walls of the corridors were lined with displays of "star graduates," photos and descriptions of their accomplishments since leaving Jianping. The ones I noticed were in computers, business, and journalism, and several had graduated from universities in the United States.

As we toured the campus, William showed us the bunk beds in the cramped dormitory room that he had shared with seven other students, the library with two floors of books which he had devoured, the track in front of the dorm where he had run every day after studying, and the gymnasium building with a basketball court upstairs that doubled as an auditorium. He also pointed to the empty lot, where the study center had once existed. It now was to be replaced by a sports facility.

He explained that as a boarding student, he was in a minority in his class. His girlfriend, for instance, lived at home with her parents, who were medical doctors in the Pudong district of Shanghai. But that did not stop William from developing a strong dose of self-confidence and embarking on a personal quest to uncover his immense potential.

By the time I met him, when he had chosen English as his university major, he was already getting restless with the course offerings at Zhejiang University and was always on the lookout for more books to read. William thrives on wide-ranging topics such as world history, philosophy, literature, travel. He has an excellent command of spoken English and proved it one evening in Shanghai when he attended his first ever live theater performance. He simultaneously interpreted an entire four-act opera for my husband and me and another visiting English professor from South Africa. The opera was sung in local Chinese dialect and subtitled with Mandarin characters.

Shaoxing opera, popularly known as Yue opera because of Shaoxing's geographic situation as belonging to the ancient state of Yue, is distinct from the more famous Peking opera. Shaoxing is a southern type of Chinese opera, whereas Peking opera is northern Chinese in style. The performance of Shaoxing opera that we attended employed female actresses only and included no acrobatics or fighting scenes. The unusually lyrical songs, although staged in traditional costumes and settings, had obvious relevance to today's society. One act told the story of an embittered poet-official who had abandoned his position in the capital city to enjoy an isolated life communing with nature in the mountains, but when summoned back to the capital could not resist the still potent desire to wield influence and power. Another act depicted a man and wife in conflict over the husband's idleness and lack of ambition. The dramatic story climaxed with the wife stabbing herself in her beautiful eyes so that her husband would never again waste time admiring her, but instead would concentrate on studying to pass the examinations for officialdom.

When I left China, William was studying hard to become fluent in Japanese and was about to start learning Italian. He had also begun to write poetry, at first translating Chinese poems into English and then composing poems of his own. Later, he tried his hand at investigative journalism by conducting personal interviews with the women who cleaned the university dorms and served the food in the cafeteria.

William was critical of much of what he observed in Chinese society: the disparity in salaries and working conditions between cleaners and professionals; compulsory 15-day universal military training, and even his fellow university students, many of whom were "boys who care about nothing but that crappy protagonist in the computer game, talk nonsense on cell phones all day long and smoke cigarettes like a dumpy ass." The seeds for much of this indignation and sense of alienation had been sown decades ago, a reflection of his unusual family background.

Family History

When we were walking together in downtown Shanghai, William pointed out the site of his mother's childhood house. "See, where the multistoried Xinhua bookstore is?" he asked. "That used to be her house, a large private family house on Fuzhou Road. In the 1950s to 1970s they shared it with other families as well, but then it was torn down in 1995." With very little urging from me, William volunteered to research his family's background. He interviewed his mother about the lives of his grandparents and wrote up in English what she reported:

> My matrilineal grandfather was born in Sichuan province in 1914. After graduating from a normal school, he had been a teacher until the outbreak of the Lugou Bridge incident in 1937. In order to fight against the Japanese Army, my grandpa dropped his pen and registered in the number 21 student troop. Transferred from the student troop during the Anti-Japanese War, he was then officially trained by the authorities in the second branch of Huangpu Military School, where he acquired the qualification of logistics officer in a regiment of the KMT Army.
>
> The whole organization was dismantled as the Anti-Japanese War was blessed with victory in 1945. The administration then placed my grandpa in a financial organization in Shanghai dealing with banking. There was an interlude after the victory over the Japanese Army when many of his colleagues chose to flee to Taiwan with the KMT. He was invited, but he remained in Shanghai, which paved another path for his family.
>
> In 1967 when the Cultural Revolution broke out, the Red Guard soldiers were seen everywhere: streets, buses, shops, houses, schools, factories and so on. Periodically, a bunch of Red Guard soldiers would break into my grandpa's house searching for ironclad evidence for prosecution while at the same time sneaking something or smashing something at will.
>
> My mother can still vaguely remember what happened. "Bunches of people rushed into the house, hailing Long Live Chairman Mao, Down with feudalism, Down with authority, and all kinds of slogans. They smashed vases and were quite rude to everyone in the house," she recollected. My grandpa couldn't escape from his heavy, laborious job, and from the preparations for the coming of the Red Guard soldiers that had to be made from time to time.
>
> He retired in 1977 and from then on he enjoyed all the practices for elderly people. According to the policy, however, if grandpa could have retired one year later, my mom would have been offered a position in the banking system and her life would have been changed forever. He died of lung cancer in 1990.

William's matrilineal grandmother was eleven years younger than his grandfather and he had personal memories of her. Only recently had she died, during summer 2005. He had returned home from YuYao in Zhejiang province, where he had been working as a teaching assistant at an English language summer camp, to attend his grandmother's "decent funeral." He wrote:

> She was born in She County, Anhui province in 1925. She came from a landlord family, whose descendants were all a little bit scholarly. Her life was rooted in She County until one day she successfully passed the matriculation and enrolled in a normal college in Shanghai, where she met my grandfather while playing table tennis. They married and my grandma bore my first uncle when she was nineteen, which was 1944.
>
> After graduation she had been serving as a teacher in a Shanghai elementary school on Nanjing East Road. She had been doing quite excellently as a teacher, winning all kinds of prizes in teaching contests held in Shanghai and respected by her colleagues as well as students. The sail of her life was fluttering against smiling sunshine before the tempest of the Cultural Revolution hit upon the whole nation. In 1967, being an excellent teacher with a family milieu of landlord, which was equated to intimacy with feudalism, my grandma was gradually degraded into an ordinary cleaner assigned to laborious and meaningless dustings and moppings.

William digressed from his mother's account and inserted his own memories from stories his grandma had related to him:

> My grandmother told me that "when the ten years of the Cultural Revolution broke out, the students were really uproarious. Stirred by the revolutionary thoughts and ideologies, they practiced pranks on several of my colleagues. Some of them put a basketful of water right above the door so that when the teacher came in, ping-dong, the water just fell and the teacher suddenly looked like a drowned rat. Sneers were universally heard in classrooms. We were always very careful, or cautious, to check before entering, whether there was any gloom atop the doors."
>
> Besides the heavy labor, she was deprived of the chance to teach; instead the students would eagerly desire to "teach" something to their teachers. Around 1977, she was rehabilitated and taught school again until the mid–1980s. The reason why she retired a bit earlier than average was because at this time, my second uncle was teaching in Jilin province. By giving up her position, my second uncle could

be called back from afar to substitute for my grandma, according to the policy.

After her retirement, she stayed at home, playing mahjong with her friends or her former colleagues and practicing Taichi as her morning exercise until she suffered an emergency illness in 2004. She spent one year in the hospital with all her organs gradually failing to function and passed away in the summer of 2005.

Sunnie

Sunnie was not one of the original volunteers to participate in my research project. I had barely noticed her sitting in the front row in one of my three early-morning writing classes. She had rarely opened her mouth during any of the one-and-half-hour-long class meetings, and I had presumed that she was one of the quiet students who were not comfortable enough speaking English to assert their opinions about the course readings.

I started to get to know her only after grading her essay called a "turning point in my life." As a teacher of English writing in China, I had quickly gotten into the habit of assigning personal topics for students to write about; I had been shocked by the copious copying from the Internet when I had asked them to hand in book reviews and even descriptions of their hometowns. This essay, therefore, was to be modeled loosely upon a class reading of a short extract entitled "Salvation" from Langston Hughes' autobiography, in which he describes a critical turning point in his life that occurred at age thirteen when he lost his faith in Jesus.

Sunnie's life-changing event was the death of her father, which had happened in December 2004, only a few months before she began my class. She wrote that the last time she had seen her father was in September 2004 at the Beijing train station, as he was waving to wish her goodbye and good luck for her junior year. Although he had been killed in a road accident while crossing the street in Beijing a few months later, Sunnie did not learn of his death until she returned home in February. Her mother and grandparents intentionally did not inform her of the tragedy, not wanting to distract her from studying and taking exams at university, she explained in her essay. But the news sent her to seek counseling at

Sunnie and her mother in doorway of their hutong in Beijing.

Zhejiang University, and she had been depressed during the entire semester. Ah, now I realized why Sunnie had remained silent in class.

The next impression I had of Sunnie was altogether different. She had asked to borrow my book, *American Women Conservationists* (McFarland 2004), a copy of which I had brought with me to China and always showed to my classes as a means of introduction. She kept the book longer than a week, during which time I happened to open the Internet site called "My Hero.com." There, to my astonishment I read the following reader comment: "I'm a Chinese student in Zhejiang University. Madelyn Holmes is my teacher this semester. I borrowed this book from her for a week. I like it very much, the women she wrote in her book were clever and brave. I think maybe I will be a conservationist in the future by her influence. However, I couldn't buy this book in China, so I cannot finish reading it." Sunnie can finish reading it now, for of course I gave her the copy I brought with me to China.

Childhood

Sunnie was born on January 22, 1984, in a historic district of Beijing, situated just south of Tian'anmen Square. As the only child in her family, she spent her childhood residing in a two-room apartment in Hou Sun Gong Yuan *hutong* with her parents, who married in 1983. A *hutong* is a traditional Chinese housing unit, many of which have become tourist attractions. They originally were constructed beginning in the Yuan dynasty (1271–1368) as the private mansions of businessmen or officials. The living space contains one-story buildings arranged around a central courtyard. After 1949, when people from the countryside flocked into Beijing, the former mansions became homes to many families. The apartment that Sunnie's family inhabits is part of an eight-family complex, where everyone knows each other and where the bathroom is a shared facility.

Her mother, who now works as the *hutong's* administrative officer, still lives there but alone after her husband's death. Sunnie's father had worked as a mechanic in a state-owned construction company, and her mother had been a house painter for almost thirty years.

Sunnie's compact home comprises a kitchen area, a bedroom, and a small living cum dining room. There is central heating and running water, a television set, telephone, and a large aquarium. Because Sunnie's father was a hobbyist taxidermist, ample space has been reserved to display an impressively stuffed eagle. When Sunnie and her mother visited our university-furnished two-and-half-room apartment in Hangzhou, they both exclaimed that they had never before seen such a large apartment.

Unprecedented transformations are now taking place in historical sections of Beijing in the throes of face-lifting in preparation for the 2008 Olympics. Sunnie's family was fearful that their *hutong* would be transformed, mindful that the neighboring *hutong*'s administrative center now houses a museum and theater for Peking opera. But Sunnie's mother has learned that their *hutong* will be spared: strands of garlic will continue to decorate their front door; potted plants and an overhanging clothesline will still clutter their tiny courtyard; SUVs, vans, sedans and bicycles will still line their narrow alleys. And the skyline of modern, multistory buildings will still stretch beyond and surround their community.

Only a few blocks from their home lies Liulichang Culture Street, which is dominated by bookstores and shops that specialize in art supplies, prints, and original works. When we visited, a landscape painter was having an opening at one of the street's handful of galleries. As a teenager, Sunnie told me, she had frequented this street after school hours, perhaps contributing to her artistic bent. Nearby, at a traditional Beijing restaurant, famous for its Qing dynasty-dressed waiters with hair hanging down their backs in long queues, her mother and she insisted on treating us to lunch.

Education

Just around the corner from the *hutong* is the primary school that Sunnie had attended. It stands four stories high and has a paved frontyard that serves as the playground. After six years at this school, Sunnie passed the exam to enter Beijing Number 15 Middle School, a key school in the south of the city and only a fifteen-minute bike ride away from her home.

She excelled in mathematics at school but was not an excessively hardworking student, although she always got high scores on examinations. She liked music and art, but explained to me that Chinese schools do not take these subjects seriously because they are not included in the college entrance exams. She made many friends among her classmates and especially appreciated a winter vacation school trip to southern China, with visits to Nanjing and Suzhou.

When it came time to apply to university, it was her father who encouraged her to apply to Zhejiang University: "I think he wanted me to experience some place different from the environment in Beijing and northern China and to become more independent and mature. I agreed with my father, because I looked forward to these differences and changes that would make university life exciting. I love travel. I love making new friends. I love exploration!"

Not until she entered university did her special interests come into focus. She took swimming lessons and became well known in the dormitory for her salsa dancing. "I like to chat," she told me, and does not consider herself as academic as her roommates, who can spend from eight in the morning until ten at night reading English novels. In fact, in high school her English was very poor. She had chosen to major in economics, but Zhejiang University did not accept her in that field but placed her in business English. "I wanted to give myself a chance to put all my effort into improving my English. I hold a bit of spirit of challenge," she admits.

She had anticipated traveling to her boyfriend's home in Urumqi in far-away Xinjiang Uygur Autonomous Region after graduation, but their romance had already broken up by the beginning of senior year. "We were constantly arguing," she confesses. Now she plans to return to work in Beijing. "I don't know what kind of job I will find, but I want to earn money for myself and my mother and to discover what I really want to do with my life. I am considering interior decoration."

Parents

Her family, at least on her mother's side, has had a proclivity for art. For several generations "painter" has been the family occupation. If Sunnie does become a decorator, she will be following in her grandfather's and her mother's footsteps, but her future life will be far removed from both her mother's and grandfather's. Her mother started out at the age of sixteen in 1973, curtailing her middle school education when her father died. As was the custom in China, a child could assume a parent's job. Sunnie's grandfather had worked as a painter for the government and had been part of the team that had painted the door of the Great Hall of the

People (Congress building) on Tian'anmen Square. Her mother's most vivid work-related memory took place in spring 1977, when she was one of the painters of the Mao Zedong mausoleum, which opened on May 1, 1977. She stayed in this occupation until she reached the age of forty-five and only recently has taken up a new position, working in the administration of her local community.

Both of Sunnie's parents were born and raised in Beijing, and her mother's side of the family can trace its ancestry back to the officialdom of the Manchu government. That means that Sunnie is part Han and part Manchu. When she graduated from high school, she and her mother traveled to the Inner Mongolia Autonomous Region to visit distant relatives. Her grandparents on her father's side of the family still live nearby, as do her mother's three sisters, one brother and all of their one-child families.

Vivian

Vivian was the other undergraduate from northern China whom I interviewed who had chosen to attend university in southern China. She

Vivian at Zhejiang University, Zijingang campus.

grew up in Zhengzhou, a large industrial city and capital of Henan province. In 1960, when U. S. journalist Edgar Snow toured Zhengzhou (written then as Chengchow), he described it as a city "being transformed" (*The Other Side of the River, Red China Today*, NY: Random House, 1961, p. 520). Before the war the city had claimed a population of 150,000, whereas when he visited, "the municipality embraced five counties with 2,800,000 inhabitants and now there were 221 modern factories" (p. 520).

Today Zhengzhou, which is situated twenty-two miles south of the Yellow River, is known as an important railway hub, home to the national grain wholesale market and to one of only three Chinese Commodity Exchanges. The city and its metropolitan area now house a populace of nearly six million. In common with other large Chinese cities, Zhengzhou has an international exhibition center, high-tech science park, downtown shopping malls, university, and archaeological remains reflecting a time of former glory. In fact, Zhengzhou can trace its history back to the beginnings of Chinese civilization in the Shang dynasty 3,500 years ago.

Childhood

Vivian was born on November 23, 1982, two years after her parents' marriage. The family lived in a small, one-room apartment in a three-story building, which was company housing for the Zhengzhou Coal Mining Machine Factory where her mother was employed. Vivian has fond memories of her childhood home and the communal life on a "close-knit apartment corridor." As an only child, she appreciated all the neighboring children of her same age and was not bothered about sharing a toilet and kitchen facilities. Eventually, while they were still living there, this apartment building was equipped with private toilets and modernized kitchens. It was not until 1997, when she was fifteen, that her family moved out into another section of the city and bought a three-room new apartment in a seven-story building.

The primary school that Vivian attended also was affiliated with her mother's place of employment. All the neighborhood children went there, just as they had all previously gone to the factory's nursery. There were thirty children in her class, but she soon stood out for academic excellence. "I always read a lot and remember reading *Gone with the Wind* in Chinese when I was nine or ten. I liked traditional Chinese novels and enjoyed listening to stories told on the radio at noon."

Her next school was Zhengzhou Foreign Language Middle School, one of China's thirteen key foreign language schools. This highly reputed school, which was built in 1982, claims that 97 percent of its graduates go on to university. Each year several students, such as Vivian, are recruited to attend Zhejiang University without taking the college entrance exam. Unlike many other undergraduates who had boarded at their middle schools, Vivian had been able to live at home because her family moved to the district in Zhengzhou where the middle school was situated. Commuting was only a twenty-minute bike ride for her.

Naturally Vivian did well in her studies and liked all the academic subjects, but decided to concentrate in science rather than arts. She admits that English was a challenge for her and a friend of her mother's tutored her. But middle school for Vivian was not all study: "I made all of my best friends at this school, and there was also time for watching films and reading."

University

At the beginning of the fall semester in 2001 Vivian departed for Hangzhou to start her university education at Zhejiang University. However, a few months later she was studying at the National University of Singapore. This chapter in her life began when her parents were sent a letter from Zhejiang University inviting their daughter to take an exam for participation in an exchange program with the National University of Singapore. Thirty-three freshmen passed the exam and left for Singapore in the winter of 2001.

For Vivian that two-year experience in Singapore was "a nightmare," the memory of which continues to haunt her. She said, "I was very lonely, sickly, and failed my courses. After studying computer engineering for only a few semesters I took medical leave, and my mother came to bring me back to China. My reaction was humiliating to me."

When I met her in my writing class during spring semester 2005, I knew that she had studied in Singapore but at first I was aware of only one effect: Vivian's English was the best in the class. Only later was I to hear about her traumatic experiences and also about her "disastrous Internet romance with an older Chinese man."

After many hours at the university's counseling services and consultations with a psychologist, she still does not understand why it was impossible for her to adjust to studying in Singapore. She finally figured out how to reconstruct her undergraduate life, however, choosing to major in business English. After I left Zhejiang University I learned that she had been accepted as a graduate student in economics. "This seemed to be a good solution for me. I like math, politics and English, and I am interested in the reform of the agricultural regions of China," she told me. As Vivian is the only undergraduate whom I met with a strong interest in the preservation of nature and the environment, this personal career choice may be of benefit to China, too. She told me that if she were accepted at the graduate school at Zhejiang University, she intended to start up a Hangzhou branch of the Friends of Nature, an environmental nongovernmental organization based in Beijing.

Family history

Vivian documented fully three generations of her family's history. Even though I never visited her hometown of Zhengzhou and never met any of her family members, she interviewed them in Chinese and then translated into English what they reported. Both her parents were born in 1955, and her maternal grandmother, who is her sole living grandparent, was born in 1933.

Because Vivian interviewed her grandmother as well as her parents, their memories of what happened in Zhengzhou and in neighboring Fengqiu county in Henan province provide a personal account of historical events beginning in the 1930s. Interviewing her grandmother was not an easy task. When Vivian approached her with my questions, her reply was "I don't remember." Vivian persevered, prodding her grandmother's memory by telling a small lie. "My teacher told me that I would fail my English class if I didn't hand in this assignment," she said, and her grandmother complied:

VIVIAN: Do you have any memory of the war with Japan?
GRANDMOTHER: I remember most clearly that Chinese were not allowed

to speak Chinese anymore under the occupation by Japan. Japanese implemented enslaving education. At that time every school had Japanese officials and teachers. The Japanese language was assigned as a major lesson from grade one. Every Monday morning people were required to worship the emperor of Japan. When Japanese invaders came to our home county, our people hated and feared them. A special person would sound a drum and gong and inform people whenever Japanese came to our village. Once hearing the sound, people would leave home and run to the fields to avoid meeting with Japanese. There was one time when some men ran a little slowly and they were seized and killed by the Japanese. Japanese invaders robbed everything they saw: food, chickens. They set houses on fire. They implemented "three all policy," which is "kill all, fire all, and rob all." They did all evils. We will never forget this period of history.

VIVIAN: Do you have recollections of the Chinese Civil War?

GRANDMOTHER: I had moved to Zhengzhou from my home county in the Civil War. At that time life was extremely hard. In my memory we felt hungry every day and the prices increased swiftly. Beggars were everywhere. Every day there were trains in the station to carry cannons and soldiers of the Kuomintang to battlefields.

VIVIAN: What is your memory of Liberation? Did it change your life?

GRANDMOTHER: It seems that it was in 1949. For several days people could hear the sound of cannons from places far away. Rumor said that the Kuomintang had been defeated by the Communist Party in war and that the Red Army was coming. One day we heard that the Red Army did come. We all ran into the streets to welcome the army. The army marched in an orderly way, with their guns on their shoulders. They looked cheerful. After Liberation, the new government encouraged women to work. I also began to work [grandmother worked at a ceiling-making factory and grandfather at a meat-processing factory]. Therefore, my family had incomes and food. Life became much better than before Liberation. I married your grandfather in January 1952 and had seven children. Your mother was the second-born.

VIVIAN: What do you remember about the 1950s and 1960s?

GRANDMOTHER: There were lots of productive and political movements in the 1950s. In 1952 our army entered Korea to help North Korea to fight with South Korea and America. In 1958 Chairman Mao started the "great leap" movement. The whole nation was called upon and stirred to make steel in order to compete with the UK and America. Famine started in late 1959 and early 1960 because of bad climate. There was not enough food. People dug wild plants to eat. Many got diseases and became bloated because of hunger. In the 1960s a new movement called "four clearing" began. The Cultural Revolution began in the late 1960s.

VIVIAN: Did your life change at work or at home during the 1970s?

GRANDMOTHER: I remember that vouchers were required to buy whatever one needed in the 1970s. There were cloth vouchers, food vouchers, candy vouchers. After the end of the Cultural Revolution I had a new job and life changed a lot [grandparents cooked pork skin from tongues and tails and sold it on a trolley in the market and in the apartment courtyard]. In the later 1970s I had my first sight of two-story buildings and TV sets. People's elementary needs for food and clothes were satisfied. Children had their opportunity of education and went to work after their education. Life is better and better.

Vivian's parents, who were born in 1955, both grew up in Zhengzhou and completed their nine years of schooling in 1973. Afterwards, they were sent to the countryside in Henan province to work as manual workers, which was the normal course for millions of teenagers during the Cultural Revolution, when China abandoned its long-held practice of offering competitive examinations for admission to university. Vivian's mother was assigned to work in a canteen, serving food to the field workers, one of whom was Vivian's father. That is when their romance began. "I kind of envy them for that period," Vivian remarked as she described her parents' courtship. "They actually had known each other in school, but my mother had been a good student and she hadn't thought much of my father at middle school. But when they were working in the countryside, my mother was subjected to bullying by her fellow workers and one day she was sitting and crying on the bank of the river. That day my father had been hunting and when he saw her sitting there, he stopped and comforted her. After that, my mother started putting bits of meat under his bowl of rice, treating him specially, a sure indication of her warm feelings for him." They married in 1980.

To Vivian, who went through adolescence during the 1990s, her parents' stint in the countryside during the 1970s may appear as romantic. But their respective career paths have never seemed enviable to her. Thwarted in her aspirations for further education, her mother joined the Zhengzhou Coal Mining Machine Factory in 1978 as an administrative worker. She worked in labor affairs, responsible for female workers and director of the office in charge of birth control. She retired in 2005 at the age of fifty, but from 1997 to 2001 had managed also to complete a university degree part-time at an engineering college in Jiaozuo, a nearby city.

In 1978, her father started his working life in the warehouse of a state-owned Zhengzhou construction company and was employed there until he was laid off in 1998. For the next three years he was unemployed, but in 2001 he and several friends formed their own small private business. They rent materials and equipment, such as scaffolds, to construction companies, and up to now it has been a successful undertaking.

Her parents' lives have changed along with China. Her mother told Vivian that "in the early 1980s only rare families could own TV sets and refrigerators, whereas nowadays every family has these facilities. People's lives are happier, more colorful and more convenient than before. We have more time to enjoy our lives with time and money to get together with families and friends, either at home or at recreational sites or by traveling."

After retirement, her mother found herself another job and is planning to join an environmental organization and contribute her effort. "I believe a whole new phase of life will start though I am not clear what it will be. At this moment I mainly focus on how to arrange my life and use my time scientifically," Vivian's mother reported.

2

Rural Students Born in the 1980s

Three students whom I interviewed grew up in China's rural areas: Wendy in Hunan province and Fan Gao and Xue Yan in Anhui province. Their childhood backgrounds differ in several ways from those of their fellow urban classmates. None is an only child, and yet they are the only children in their families to attend university. They excelled in their studies at school, whereas none of their parents had received much formal education. They are studying at Zhejiang University with financial assistance from the government.

Wendy

Wendy, a conscientious student, was one of the first to volunteer to participate in my research project. Although short in height, as are most female undergraduates, she could not be described as petite but rather as athletically built. She was born on July 6, 1984, in Sai hui village in Bai mu township in Hunan province. Her home is situated near the city of Loudi and is not far distant from the birthplace of Mao Zedong in Shaoshan. This southern interior province is known as China's main rice-producing area, but the hilly terrain is also suitable for the growing of fruit. Seedless Hunan tangerines are a provincial specialty.

Childhood

The first house that Wendy occupied with her family was small and old, with one room that served as the kitchen and living room and another room that was furnished with two beds. They stayed in this dwelling until 1996, when Wendy turned twelve, even though her younger brother had been born in 1987. China's one-child policy allowed for rural couples to have a second child if the first-born was a girl.

The new house that her family built in the mid–1990s has two stories and is quite modern, according to Wendy's description. Yet, a well still supplies the family's water, and there is no indoor toilet. This house has many rooms: a large multipurpose room, two bedrooms, a separate kitchen, a living room, a bathroom and a storage area on the second floor. Outside in the front yard the family has set up an altar shrine. Household chickens freely congregate in the yard.

Both her parents, who were born in the 1950s, work as farmers on the small family plots of rice and vegetables. Her paternal family can trace its roots on this land back many generations, and her grandfather held positions of leadership in the administration of the village for many years. Most of the villagers belong to a single family grouping with the same surname as Wendy's. During class discussions of Alex Haley's book *Roots*, Chinese students mentioned that African and Chinese villages shared the same tradition of linking names for geographical places with family surnames. Author Haley had tracked down the village from which his slave ancestor originated because he knew the name of the family clan.

The village that Wendy called home had changed markedly since 1949. Agricultural production had been collectivized with the creation of producers' cooperatives and later People's Communes in the late 1950s, and the "iron rice bowl" system that guaranteed lifelong healthcare, housing, education, and social security had transformed traditional village society. By the time Wendy was born in 1984, however, the communal fields in her village had been divided into family plots and the household responsibility system that encouraged farmers to maximize output had already been introduced. During Wendy's childhood the collectivized support sys-

Wendy at Zhejiang University, Zijingang campus.

tem was abandoned, and thereafter villagers were charged fees for the provision of social services.

Education

The primary school that Wendy attended was situated in another village, a fifteen-minute walk from her home. She did well at school from an early age and remembers other children always begging her for answers to arithmetic problems. Her next school was a middle school in Bai mu township. It was an hour away from her house, which meant that she commuted by bus. Here she started to learn English and was active in sports, especially ping pong, badminton and basketball.

In contrast to her younger brother, who dropped out of school, Wendy completed her pre-university education at a government-financed boarding school in the city of Loudi. She boarded for three years, returning to her village only once a month. Her favorite subject in high school was mathematics.

She was not homesick for her family, she told me, because she spent her weekends with her uncle, who worked at the local steel company. Loudi, although home to a major state-run steel enterprise, remains a small-sized city with an urban population of 140,000. Perennial problems with flooding have limited the city's expansion, but a substantial flood-control project is now in the works. The city government, touting its ambition to become a major transport hub and distribution center in southern China, has already set its sights on increased trade with and investment from the state of Minnesota in the USA. In March 2006 a Chinese delegation visited the Twin Cities of St. Paul–Minneapolis to establish an office there to be operated by a full-time staff person from Loudi.

When Wendy passed the college entrance examination and was accepted at Zhejiang University, she earned the respect of her community. As she puts it, they "spoke highly of me." Altogether, only three other people from her village have gone to university.

University student

As a student at Zhejiang University, Wendy selected business English as her major with the intention of doing post-graduate study in international finance. Her predominant interest pertains to management, and she chose to write for the class assignment "my hero" about a student leader whose group management skills she admires. But her final essay, entitled "The Year 1992," reflects more broadly her philosophy of life:

The year 1992 is a milestone in China's economic history. Since 1992, the Chinese people have stepped steadily and confidently onto a new marketing economic road, a promising developing road. All the Chinese people will remember this year 1992 and thank the grand old man Deng Xiaoping who made an inspection tour to South China in January 1992 at almost 88 years old....

Under the background of an unfavorable global situation and the suspicious atmosphere inside the country, some Chinese people began to doubt our policy. Deng Xiaoping's speech, like a wind to blow away the clouds, answered common people's doubting questions and gave a logical and brilliant answer to academic scholars and politicians about China's future. He pointed out that economic development was the only way for China's future and socialist China could adopt a market economy. In addition, he gave confidence to foreign investors and economic constructors....

Due to Deng Xiaoping's persuasive views and theories in 1992, China continued to deepen the reforming and opening up process smoothly. Since the solution of ideological problems China has stridden onto a healthy and fast-developing highway.

Very few of my students were as committed to economic reform or as interested in it as was Wendy. Perhaps the reason lay in her own roots. She had come from a rural area in Hunan province, which was Mao Zedong's home province, and had staunchly supported the Cultural Revolution. Consequently, this region of China had been late to adopt reforms. As a child growing up in the 1990s, remote from the dynamism of the urban eastern seaboard, Wendy embraced wholeheartedly the new ideas and prospects made available to her at university in prospering Hangzhou. She was especially receptive to the forging of a post–Maoist Chinese economy and society, appreciative of the philosophy of Deng Xiaoping and supportive of the reforms that he had initiated.

Two Students from Anhui Province

Anhui province, which neighbors Zhejiang, where Hangzhou is situated, was home to Fan Gao and Xue Yan, although their families live in distinct regions of the same province. Fan Gao comes from a southern mountainous district, where rice is the staple crop. His village is only eight hours by bus from Hangzhou and has more affinity with the province of Zhejiang than with Anhui. He has never visited the provincial capital city of Hefei. In contrast, Xue Yan's home is in the flatlands in the northern part of the province, where wheat is cultivated and the climate is more temperate. For her undergraduate education she attended Anhui University in Hefei, and she chose Zhejiang University in the much larger city of Hangzhou for graduate studies. The differences between northern and southern Anhui province are so pronounced that when the People's Republic of China was founded in 1949, the two regions were governed by separate administrative authorities, which were merged into one province only in 1952.

Compared to the adjacent provinces of Zhejiang and Jiangsu to the east, Anhui has always been a poor cousin in terms of economic development and per capita income. Its fame resides in its maintenance of ancient Chinese tradition. In the southern region of the province, especially in the city and vicinity of Huizhou, where merchants had established thriving commercial activities during the Ming and Qing dynasties, large numbers of ancient buildings have been well-preserved. Contemporary residents continue to produce the so-called four treasures of literary pursuits, namely ink sticks and slabs, *xuan* paper and writing brushes. Mount Jiuhua, one of China's four famous Buddhist sanctuaries, is situated in Anhui, as is Mount Huangshan (Yellow Mountain), which enjoys a well-deserved reputation as one of the ten major scenic attractions of China.

Fan Gao

When Fan Gao volunteered to participate in my research project he told me why: he wanted to see how someone went about writing a book, because his ambition is to become a writer. During the course of the semester I became well aware that he could write excellent English essays, but not until the last class meeting did I realize that he also is a talented poet. He is slight in build with a narrow face and thick-lens glasses to compensate for weakness in vision. His keen intelligence and exceptional abilities might conjure up an image of a nerd, but he was amiable, had many friends and as he put it, "I can adapt easily."

This portrait will diverge from the others in this book in two ways. It will include a graphic description of his farm and extended family based on my visit to his home in the Yellow Mountains of Anhui province. I also am reprinting four poems that he wrote in English and which were published in a Zhejiang University poetry magazine that he helped to found in 2006.

Childhood

Fan Gao was born on July 31, 1984, in a village adjacent to Sankou, a small town approximately forty minutes by bus from the national scenic area and UNESCO World Heritage site, Huangshan (Yellow Mountain). Fan Gao is the youngest of three children; his sister (now 29) and his brother (now 26) were both born before the implementation of China's one-child policy. His parents, who are in their mid-to-late-fifties, have worked as farmers on the same land during their entire lives. They have seen the rice fields change hands three times: from landlord/peasant land ownership in the 1940s, to communal landholdings in the 1950s, and to the introduction of a household responsibility system or individual small plots in the 1980s.

The two-story brick farmhouse that the family built twelve years ago is situated on the same lot as the smaller, stucco house in which Fan Gao lived as a child. His family's house is spacious, with four large rooms downstairs and a storage area on the second floor, and it is equipped with electricity, telephone service, and satellite television. In contrast to these twentieth-century amenities, there is no piped water, no refrigerator nor any other kitchen appliance. Bathroom facilities do not exist. I had to ask his mother via Fan Gao's interpretation, "Please, can I use the bucket?" and then embarrassedly announce, "Thank you, I am finished," and watch his mother remove it from the bedroom where I slept. To prepare a bath, his mother would carry a large basin to the dining room table and fill it with water from the outside well that she had heated on the wood-burning kitchen stove.

The farmhouse faces onto a beautiful rural scene, with low hills in the distance and a magnificent clear view of stars at night. The rice fields lie about one-quarter mile from the house, with access via dirt paths wide enough to accommodate motorcycles but not cars. Fan Gao's parents use only bicycles, a cart, and their two feet to get around, but everyone else travels in and out on noisy motorcycles while fending off the barking dogs that belong to the neighbors. Here, with a large household garden in the front yard, with pigs and chickens in the backyard, and a cow tethered to a post in the small wooded hillside above, Fan Gao grew up. And here is also where his childhood friend and neighbor, who now is studying engineering at university, grew up. His family lives among a cluster of traditional grey and white, southern Anhui-style houses located just across the front garden from Fan Gao's.

This rural area, where fertile arable land continues to be cultivated and long-held patterns of living are still retained, may not remain that way for long. None of the children in Fan Gao's family will continue this lifestyle, and tourist development for the nearby national scenic area is encroaching upon this area. Much of the view clearly visible from the bus window as we left the rocky cliffs of Yellow Mountain until we approached the small town of Sankou consists of new hotels, clusters of modern houses, bridges, tunnels, and road construction. To my surprise, Fan Gao, who had grown up neighboring this world-class natural site, had never ventured up the mountain nor viewed its renowned sunrise, as have millions of tourists from China and around the globe.

According to Chinese governmental planning, the prioritizing of development is supposed to improve the economic well-being of rural areas. In the case of Yellow Mountain in southern Anhui province, the spectacular natural scenery with its ancient pine trees, fantastically-shaped rocks, seas of clouds, and hot springs is the area's leading attribute. Expanding facilities for tourists will necessarily displace farming communities but if carried out with care may not destroy the natural wonder. How can I write such a statement in the face of China's uncountable rural development projects, many of which have ignited national and international environmental controversies?

The reason for my reserved optimism about the future of Yellow Mountain is because of the already established tourist facilities there, which are the best I observed in China. The size of the mountain park is huge (154 square kilometers), but as one of China's top ten tourist attractions the number of visitors is also huge. When I visited I had to stand in line for three hours to ride up on one of the three cable cars. Once up among the peaks the trails are not crowded, in striking contrast to the Great Wall, for instance; the air is pure; the shops and hotels do not dominate the scene; and best of all the trash bins are continually emptied by a crew of 500 workers.

Of course, the sight is magnificent, as has been noted for thousands of years by poets, scientists, and travelers. At Yellow Mountain, where every view looks like it comes straight out of a landscape painting, the traditional Chinese concept of combining man and nature is given full play. Trails are not dirt paths through the woods, but stone steps built to ease the climbing, with railings and benches placed at optimal vantage points. Even sedan chairs are available for the weak or disabled. The shapes of the stones are given names (turtle peak, an immortal walking on stilts, lotus-flower peak, squirrel jumping on the celestial capital peak), as are the pine trees (harp, dragon claws, playing chess, greeting guest). Trailside markers display excerpts from Tang dynasty–era poems, and guides with megaphones inform their tour groups about the names humans have attached to pine trees and mountains. When I reached the top of Lotus Peak at 1873 meters, a primary-school teacher asked me in English, "What do you think about the view?" He told me that it made him proud of China.

The granite mountains with their peculiar shapes are home to 1500 species of plants, contributing to their attraction to scientists as well as to health enthusiasts. According to Taoist beliefs, the first man to make use of the mountain's medicinal herbs was the legendary Yellow Emperor of the third millennium B.C., ancestor to all Chinese people. When he reached the age of 480, reputedly he climbed up this mountain in order to find plants that would make him immortal. He concocted pills made from plant leaves, swallowed several and flew up to heaven. This story affected Tang dynasty Emperor Xuanzong so strongly that in 747 A.D. he changed the name of the mountain from *Yishan* (black mountain) to *Huangshan* (yellow mountain) in honor of the Yellow Emperor.

Education

The first school that Fan Gao attended, a long, white one-story building with black shingle roofing, was close to his house and up a short path from the rice fields. When I visited, the building was no longer used as a primary school, but posted above and below the blackboard that was still hanging on the front wall were bold, red Chinese characters proclaiming the government's one-child policy. Now the former school building houses Fan Gao's former teacher, who came out into his vegetable garden to greet me. With Fan Gao interpreting, he explained that he had started teaching there in 1975, but because there were fewer and fewer children in the village, the school had closed its doors in 2002. When Fan Gao was his student in the early 1990s, there were only ten children in his class that included grades one to three. This man still teaches primary school but walks to a school twenty minutes away in Sankou town. As soon as I was introduced to him, he pointed to Fan Gao and indicated with "thumbs up" gesturing and in basic Chinese language that he had been his best student. "*Hen hao* [excellent]," he asserted.

Fan Gao had learned to read before starting school. His sister taught him reading, and his brother taught him math. As he recalls, it was not until he was fifteen and had access to a high school library that he began to read literary works.

After attending the village school for three years, he went on to Sankou primary and Sankou middle school, where he started to study English. He then took the high-school entrance examination and entered Huangshan High School, where he boarded for three years. This school, with 1800 students, provided the only option for rural children eager to continue their academic schooling beyond the compulsory nine years of formal education. His neighbor went there as did his younger cousin, who grew up in Sankou. The dormitory room accommodated twelve students in one room. Only half the student body passed the college-entrance exams that would enable them to continue their education at universities.

Fan Gao excelled at this school, winning prizes in mathematics in his first and second years and graduating as class valedictorian. At the end of the second year, he chose to concentrate in humanities rather than science, influenced perhaps by his young Chinese literature teacher. "She loaned me books to read," he remembers, "and encouraged me to write creatively. I wrote two short pieces of fiction while at this school."

In early June 2002 Fan Gao, along with millions of other students around China, took the university entrance exam. He selected Zhejiang University as his first choice, out of respect for his mother's wishes that he stay near to home. Hangzhou is only eight hours away from his village, whereas Beijing, for example, is much further distant. He passed the exam, won a 2,000 *yuan* ($250) scholarship and was honored at a dinner at his school. He entered Zhejiang University without paying anything for the first year and enrolled as an English major. He admits that he had preferred to study law, as had many of my other students, but choice of major is determined by the scores received on the entrance exam. Law is more popular than English, it would seem, but for Fan Gao, who "wanted to learn about Western culture and literature," English appears to have been a fortuitous decision.

He has specialized in modern literature, writing research papers on T.S. Eliot and James Joyce, and has completed all the university's requirements, including physical education, science, Chinese composition, philosophy, and three years of politics courses. "We always skip this class because it's boring — Mao's thought, Marx's economics and Deng Xiaoping's — we have heard this already at all other levels of school." He selected Japanese as his second foreign language, and to fulfill the requirements for English majors spent one summer vacation assisting at an English camp for ten-year-olds. During another summer vacation he stayed on campus for the compulsory 15-day universal military training, where "we mostly marched but also learned how to shoot."

Like most of his classmates, Fan Gao is uncertain about his future. Because he really appreciates English literature, he at first thought that he would go on to graduate school. I asked him why he preferred to study English rather than Chinese literature, and he replied without hesitation, "I don't think twentieth-century Chinese literature is very good; it is not mature, for it has been only twenty-five years since the Cultural Revolution." He went on to explain that there is a gap between various literary styles, and that contemporary writers simplify or even imitate Ming- and Qing-dynasty novels. When pressed for a name of a recent Chinese book that he liked, he mentioned only one: *Fortress Besieged* by Ch'ien Chung-shu, which was published originally in 1947 and recently reissued to Chinese popular acclaim.

During the fall semester of his senior year he changed his mind about his career plans. "I have been a student all my life, and I really want to experience something else," he told me. "I will try to get a job that will make use of English."

Fan Gao still dreams of becoming a writer and has started writing short stories in English. An argument essay he handed in during my class, criticizing an assigned reading, "Social Responsibility in Science and Art" by British author Alex Comfort, provides an indication of his art for art's sake attitude to literature. Fan Gao titled his essay "Literary Freedom":

> Social labor is divided into different fields, assigned to different work-men and workwomen. Different people in different fields take different responsibilities in society. For example, biologists are responsible for biology, sociologists for sociology, psychologists for psychology, and the problems of environmental pollution should be exposed by environmentalists, though if a writer discovers the art in this issue, he can write a poem, essay or fiction on it.
>
> According to *The New Oxford Dictionary of English*, literature is "written works, especially those considered of superior or lasting artistic merit." *Encyclopedia Americana* also says that "Like fine music and art, fine literature is characterized by imagination, meaningfulness of expression, and good form and technique." So the essence of literature is artistry rather than social responsibility. Like the necessity of academic freedom, autonomy and neutrality, writers also need literary freedom, autonomy and neutrality to write great works.
>
> The writer should write what emerges naturally from his inside, without external pressures. Literature is not like milk, which is drawn from cows by others. Any works forced out by external pressures including social responsibility couldn't be fine ones. For example, corruption is a very serious problem in modern China. A lot of writers take this social responsibility and write many novels to uncover those corrupt officials. Those novels have proved to be low. There are many writers in history, such as Henry David Thoreau and Marcel Proust, who are outcasts from society. But society finds what they write popular. Perhaps society is attracted by a literary escapism from reality. Because when a writer escapes from the society, what he writes is truly what he thinks in his mind.
>
> Literature shows concern for permanent motifs, such as conflicts between man and nature, love of land, and the cruelty of destiny. Social responsibilities are always changing. In the reading curriculum in the USA all children read *Huckleberry Finn*. But on every other page Huckleberry is smoking tobacco, so from the social responsibility aspect, Twain's books encourage tobacco use. But in Mark Twain's day, no one understood that tobacco was harmful.
>
> Before people have time to contemplate those changing social responsibilities they may no longer be present social responsibilities. Literature is not news. It must have some permanent values. People don't expect to throw away a literary book like a newspaper as soon as they have finished reading it. People wish to put literary books on their bookshelves, reading them now and then to grasp their deep thoughts and exquisite artistic techniques. The

writer has to meditate on a matter for a long time to form a deep thought before he expands it to a poem, essay, drama or a fiction. So the matter must remain with people for long enough to allow writers to ponder over it. Most so-called social problems don't have this characteristic. For example, SARS in China 2003, Tsunami in Indonesia 2004, and the death of Pope John Paul in the Vatican 2005 could only be subjects for newspapers, magazines and the Internet. They took place too suddenly and lasted for too short a time to be fine themes for literary works. Maybe some years later, some writer may ponder over them for long and find some permanent values in them and write a great literary work. But they won't be social responsibilities any more in that "some years later."

In 2006, Fan Gao made some headway toward his ambition to become a published writer. A South African poet came to teach at Zhejiang University and, impressed by Fan Gao's abilities, invited him to co-edit a bilingual poetry journal called *Mouse*, to be published by the School of International Studies. Several of Fan Gao's poems are reprinted below. When my husband read these poems, he thought the images were too good to be original: "I bet he just translated some traditional Chinese poems. Anyway, nobody writes about sunsets and people riding on cows any more." But Fan Gao's home is in a beautiful natural area, where you can still see oxen and where people fish for the evening meal in the local stream. He told me that when he first arrived at the brand new Zijingang campus of Zhejiang University, with its twenty-first century buildings, trimmed lawns and transplanted trees, where he would have to live and study for four years, he burst into tears. Fan Gao would, and did, write compellingly about the natural rural environment.

Poems (reprinted from *Mouse*, publication of English department, School of International Studies, Zhejiang University, No.1, 2006):

Fishing

Sitting on the land,
I angle for fish in the water.

I pull up the rod.
A fish glides through the air.

A short arc,
encompasses water, air, and land.

Sunset

Rosy clouds redden the whole universe.
No doubt the two brothers, heaven and earth,
    are not good drinkers.
Holding glasses in their hands,
    they flush.

Drunkenly they lose their way,
stumble into the gloom.

The Shadow

A cow bears a herd boy on its back,
who bears the setting sun.

The sun draws out the shadow of the cow
and that of the boy.

The boy cracks a whip;
the cow flicks its tail,
flinging the sun below the horizon,

leaving the whole world
in darkness
and shadow.

Rain

Garrulous gods in heaven
Spatter saliva,
Which treks a long way
Into thoughts on the land.

The thinker says:
The clamor of human beings disturbs God,
Who quells the land with flooding.

After I left China, I learned that Fan Gao, together with an Englishman, Mark Amy, had founded a translation company named Chinese Concept. Since its establishment in February 2006 in Nanjing, the start-up firm has translated more than one million words from Chinese into English and from English into Chinese. At the beginning of 2007 their Website, chineseconcept.com, claimed a daunting list of clients that included companies in the automobile, chemical, pharmaceutical, real estate, cosmetics, engineering, financial, and electronics industries. They have also translated letters, questionnaires, newspaper articles, doctoral dissertations, and legal documents.

Family

During my visit to Fan Gao's home, I was able to interview family members ranging in age from 8 to 82: parents, grandmother, brother, sister, and aunt and uncle with their two children. Fan Gao did all the interpreting from Chinese to English.

Fan Gao looks very much like his father. Both are tall and very thin; however, the son wears glasses and the father has very brown legs, both reflections of their roles in life. His father, who was born in 1947, has worked outside as a farmer all his life. During the one day I spent at his family's home, Fan Gao's father was busy from 6:00 A.M. until dark, beginning before dawn with a drive to Sankou on his bicycle-pedaled cart. He harvested vegetables, constructed bedding for the pig stable out of bamboo and straw, cared for the cow, shucked corn, and climbed a stepladder to the second floor to retrieve supplies and tools for his various tasks. I visited in August, and Fan Gao told me that in a few weeks his parents would harvest the first rice crop from their six-*mu* (one-acre) farm. Now they plant only two crops a year, but in the past they had planted three.

He also showed me the rice mill beside the fields, now managed by an elderly woman, where his parents process the harvested rice before selling it. All the farm work — seeding, weeding, spraying, fertilizing, and harvesting — had been managed by the commune before the early 1980s, when the communal land was divided into individual family plots. Today there are fewer rice farmers in this village, and his father, who had once been a village administrator, has long since given up that responsibility.

Fan Gao wears glasses and his father does not. After only three years of primary school education, his father never mastered enough Chinese characters to be able to read fluently. As one of four children and the eldest son, he had found it necessary to begin his working life at the age of twelve, after his father's premature death in 1959. Fan Gao's grandfather had succumbed to starvation, an unfortunate victim of the famine disaster that devastated China from 1959 to 1961.

His mother, who was born in 1951, is also slightly built, but is shorter than Fan Gao and her husband. Her short black hair is not yet graying, and, dressed in long pants and a short-sleeved blouse, she appeared still youthful. But when she returned from the nearby pond, carrying double buckets on a pole over her shoulder, she looked like the hard-working farmer's wife that she has been since 1975 when she married. She spent the entire day working, but her activities varied considerably from her husband's; hers revolved primarily around food preparation. She began by slaughtering a chicken and then started up the wood-burning stove to prepare rice gruel for breakfast. Throughout the day, she was either sitting on the floor cutting up meat and spices, collecting vegetables from the garden, feeding the animals, washing and hanging clothes, or else cooking eggs and sweet corn to provide everyone with continual snacks.

Fan Gao's mother completed six years of schooling, having grown up in Sankou and not in the village. Her father had operated a pharmacy and she was the eldest of three children. After her father died in 1979, her younger sister took over the family business.

I also met Fan Gao's paternal grandmother. She does not live all the time with his parents, but rotates between the houses of her four children. She is 82 years old and walks with the aid of a cane, the result of a fall last year that affected her hip. She still wears her mostly black hair pulled back away from her face and hanging down to her shoulders, and although her skin is very wrinkled, she does not appear as frail as her years would lead you to expect. She explained apologetically that she could not help Fan Gao's mother much since her fall. Nonetheless, she still was able to take short strolls around the village and pass by the Buddhist shrine near the house every day. She also could appreciate looking at the photos of my 85-year-old mother that I had brought along, and commented that my mother looked younger than she. I replied that she had more teeth than my mother.

Fan Gao is the youngest of three children; his older sister and brother were born in 1977 and 1980 respectively. They represent an older generation in some sense, for neither of them studied at university and both have settled down in the same rural area where they grew up. His sister completed nine years of compulsory education but has never been employed. She married a local man who works as a carpenter and has a four-year-old son. Fan Gao brought his nephew a present from Hangzhou: a storybook in Chinese of Hans Christian Andersen's and the Grimm brothers' fairy tales.

His brother, who is only four years older than he, attended a local vocational college and has found a job in a construction design company in a nearby small city, where he now resides. He stayed overnight at his parents' house when I visited, and before driving his motorcycle to work plucked the feathers off the chicken which his mother was preparing to cook for dinner. He has not been working at this three-man firm for very long, but says that he likes his job even though he has to go to the office seven days a week. Previously, he had tried life as a migrant worker in Shanghai but didn't like it. He complained that "they were arrogant there and looked down on anyone who wasn't from Shanghai."

As a Chinese migrant worker, Fan Gao's brother had joined a very large labor migration, perhaps the largest in world history. There were more than 140 million migrant workers in China in 2005, according to figures released by the Chinese Academy of Social Sciences (*China Daily* online, January 29, 2007). The vast majority is comprised of rural residents who leave their homes to work in China's fast-growing cities. This extremely high rate of urbanization causes problems for both the cities to which they migrate and the workers themselves. Because of a decades-old household registration system, these migrant workers are not accorded the full rights of urban residents. They not only exist on low wages and live in temporary housing, but they also do not enjoy resident access to schools for their children and other social benefits. The process of reforming the system has begun, with Shanghai as one of several cities that have adopted a type of "green card" enabling long-term inhabitants to obtain resident status.

His brother had accompanied Fan Gao to Hangzhou when Fan Gao began his studies at Zhejiang University, and Fan Gao still asks for his advice when planning for the future. "He thinks that I should come back to this area to work," Fan Gao told me. When I returned from Yellow Mountain, which I explored with Fan Gao and two younger cousins of his, I asked his brother whether he was envious of our adventure, which he had to skip because of his job. His reply was "not really." Even though he had never been there, visiting the world-famous site held no interest for him. Observing the mountain from below satisfied his curiosity.

In addition to meeting Fan Gao's immediate family, I also interviewed his mother's sister and her husband and their two children, who reside in Sankou. This aunt is fourteen years younger than Fan Gao's mother and lives a life that in sociological parlance could be called upwardly mobile. Her lifestyle accords with the rising standard of living in today's China. The two sisters and their two families, however, maintain very close bonds, seeing one another almost daily. When I was there, his aunt spent one whole day assisting her sister in preparing the evening meal.

Fan Gao's aunt and uncle run a small business. They operate a private pharmacy on the main street of Sankou, a town of 10,000, which is twenty minutes' walking distance from Fan Gao's village. Their shop is located in the front room of a two-story house that they had built twelve years ago. They have run this drugstore, in which they sell both Chinese traditional and Western medicines, for a long time, and two years ago they paid the government to privatize it. In the vicinity other pharmacies exist that are connected to the hospital and clinics, but theirs directly serves the townspeople as well as the doctors at the medical facilities. They open every day at 6:00 A.M., and when I was there people arrived continually requesting small bags of hand-measured medicaments, which his aunt put together by reaching into the drawers behind the counter on one side of the room. On the opposite side of the room, across from the traditional Chinese medicines, glass shelves display Western ointments, cough remedies, and even the tiny Chinese-made aspirin that I bought. They still use a scale and abacus, but his uncle was eagerly anticipating learning how to transfer sales accounting to a computer that he would be installing in September.

Directly in front of the shop stands a pomegranate tree bursting with fruit, and a stream flows along the entire stretch of main street. This stream is the centerpiece for a wide array of activities. It was a very hot day when I arrived, and I watched with amazement as young children swam on inner tubes in the murky water, while women washed clothes and vegetables, and an old man harvested water plants, presumably to cook. "That is where I learned to swim," said the pharmacists' strapping, nineteen-year-old son who was soon to start teacher training at an Anhui provincial university.

In contrast to the scene at the communal stream, the house appeared to be a surprising combination of Western and Eastern features. It was filled with modern accoutrements, such as a living room with wooden furniture, a synthesizer keyboard, a large television set, upstairs bedrooms, a dog house, a separate kitchen with running water at a sink, a bathroom with tub, two toilets (one Western that only I used and one Chinese). Yet, because this area is part of southern Anhui province, the design reflects the traditional Huizhou style of architecture. That is, there is an open courtyard in the center of the house, within which lies a sunken basin where rain water collects.

Here in the courtyard the family gathers to eat their meals and afterwards congregates around the basin to wash dishes and to brush teeth.

Fan Gao's uncle, who is older than his wife, was born in 1956 and completed his nine years of schooling during the Cultural Revolutionary period in the 1970s. He then fulfilled the required two years of labor in the countryside, after which the government assigned him to work at a drugstore, offering him what would become his lifetime vocation. He even met Fan Gao's aunt, whom he married in 1986, at a drugstore. They both learned the pharmacy trade on the job, for his wife had acquired her initial familiarity with drugs while working at her family's store, and each has taken supplementary training courses at the Anhui medical school. Now they are interested in modernizing their business. He travels around on a $600 motorcycle, the second one that he has owned, and is anxious for his son to teach him how to use a computer.

The couple paid the government $1,235 in order to have a second child in 1998, a girl who is being raised quite differently from her older brother, who was born in 1986. As soon as I arrived at their house, the girl performed several tunes for me on her synthesizer keyboard. She has been taking private music lessons for one year and can read music with do re mi notation. Fan Gao's aunt and uncle have begun to travel by bus and train and have already taken their daughter with them on a week's holiday to Xi'an. His aunt, who had never before ventured outside of Anhui province, enthusiastically described the impressive cultural relics that they had visited there.

But they live in rural China, so that Fan Gao's uncle plucked the duck that his wife cooked for dinner, went out to fish, and took care of the dog as well as manning the counter at the drugstore. Fan Gao's aunt not only dealt out traditional Chinese medicine and consulted and advised her customers, but also washed, cleaned and cooked for her family and assisted her older sister. The aunt's mother-in-law also lives in the house. After each meal the mother-in-law quickly cleared away the dishes and started on the washing up.

Xue Yan

I first met Xue Yan, a shy and self-effacing young woman who is larger than her mostly petite classmates, as a student in my graduate course called Culture and History in American Literature. She signed up for my class at the start of her two-year studies for a master's degree in English literature. She had just arrived in Hangzhou from her rural village in northern Anhui province, having graduated in July as an English major from Anhui University. Later she told me that she had done so well on the graduate entrance examination that she did not have to pay tuition at Zhejiang University. As I became better acquainted with her during the course of the fall semester, I realized how impressive her academic achievements had been in the light of the huge divide that exists between Xue Yan, her parents, her siblings, and her beloved grandmother.

Childhood

Xue Yan was born on December 24, 1983, in Wangdianzi village in Funan county, which is in the northwestern section of Anhui province near to the border with the province of Henan. At the time of Xue Yan's birth her mother, whose marriage had been arranged by a broker, had already given birth to two sons, one in 1980 and the other in 1981. Both parents have been farmers all their lives, growing wheat, corn, and vegetables and raising pigs, chickens, and dogs. In recent years her mother also has started a small retail business in the village, selling cloth goods (curtains, tablecloths, quilts) that she buys wholesale in the nearest city. Her mother, who was born in 1957, never attended school, and her father, who was born in 1955, completed primary school only.

In contrast to her brothers, both of whom dropped out of school, Xue Yan always excelled in her studies and went off to boarding school in the regional city of Fuyang after finishing primary and junior middle school. She lived in the house of a relative in Fuyang while attending a key high school, which prepared her for the college-entrance examination. This city, which is about two hours from her village, lies in the middle of a rich agricultural area well known for livestock raising and the production of grain, cotton, and ingredients for traditional Chinese drugs. In addition, leather, medicine, chemicals, textiles, and electro-machinery industries have grown up there, developed for the most part as offshoots from the processing of agricultural and industrial raw materials.

Even though Xue Yan is the only university-educated member of her family, she continues to maintain very close ties with her siblings and their

Xue Yan at Zhejiang University, Zijingang campus.

children. Both of her brothers are married, and Xue Yan looks forward to playing with her two nieces and two nephews whenever she returns home for festivals or vacations. She enjoys teaching them English and how to play card games, but not sports, as she admits that she has never been particularly athletic. One brother works for a relative transporting goods between Shanghai and Guangdong, while the other brother is a bus conductor on a coach that plies the route between Hangzhou and her hometown. She rode in that coach when she first arrived in Hangzhou.

University

Xue Yan's embarking for Hefei in fall 2001 to study English at Anhui University marked the first major breakaway from her rural family. Because she had resided with a relative during high school, the experience at university, where she shared a dormitory room with seven classmates and attended classes on a campus with 14,000 students in an unfamiliar capital city, presented an array of new challenges. But she continued to excel in her studies and enjoyed shopping in downtown Hefei with her classmates. Anhui University has a strong foreign-language division, and while an undergraduate Xue Yan started studying French, along with her studies in English language and literature. She wrote a senior thesis on Thomas Hardy's *Tess d'Urbevilles*.

Perhaps as a result of her background, she was constantly self-critical when comparing herself to others. She complained that her spoken English trailed behind her reading knowledge. "I did very well on written examinations in Hefei and was therefore accepted in the postgraduate program here. But my oral skills are very weak. Indeed I have had little opportunity to practice the spoken language," she would enunciate flawlessly in English. When I met her, she felt that she needed to supplement her vocabulary in English by memorizing idioms to enliven her speaking.

Xue Yan's world expanded in all directions when she arrived in the urban metropolis of Hangzhou in fall 2005. Never before had she been to a city of six million people. Never before had she met people from the south of China or eaten southern Chinese cuisine. Never before had she seen such a beautiful natural site as West Lake, and never before had she spoken with foreign professors.

However, she coped, and the term paper she handed in for my course was the most intellectually challenging out of the total batch of twenty-five. She compared the story "Spring Silkworms," written by Mao Dun in 1932, with the novel *The Jungle*, written by Upton Sinclair in 1905. Both writers present vivid portrayals of characters who are victims of poverty perpetrated by the societies in which they dwell. In her essay Xue Yan managed to discuss how these two writers, whose societies were worlds apart from each other geographically, economically, and socially, still used similar writing techniques to create powerful pieces of literature.

After reading predominantly British authors as an undergraduate, Xue Yan decided to write her master's dissertation on the Chinese-American author Amy Tan. I realized as a teacher of English in China that students were fascinated by the history and culture of Chinese immigrants in the United States. American writers Amy Tan and Maxine Hong Kingston enjoyed considerable readership among university students.

After I left Zhejiang University to return to the United States, I received news by email from Xue Yan of yet another way in which her world had expanded: "I began to be a English teacher in the evening at Zhejiang University, and I can make a living by myself. I am so happy and so proud!" After receiving a master's degree in 2007, she plans to return to Hefei to search for a job teaching English at an institution of higher education.

Beyond Xue Yan's academic achievements, I remember most strongly her devotion to her family and especially to her paternal grandmother. When we were strolling together along West Lake, she talked about how she wished that her grandmother could see this site. When we hiked through the bamboo forest, she talked about the crops that her grandmother had grown. When we passed by a sculpture of a famous writer, she remembered that as a child her grandmother had retold her his stories:

> My grandma is a strong-willed woman and I have learned a lot from her, except for one thing: she is domineering while I am obedient. Aha, perhaps that's because she is always ready to do everything for me. Although she is 74 years old, she still likes to dominate everything in the household. And because of her unshakable insistence, our family still retains many traditional customs, and of course has not been split up into nuclear families. But I respect her awfully and love her much.

Grandmother

I was unable to travel the fourteen hours from Hangzhou to Xue Yan's village, but I asked her whether she would be willing to interview her grandmother for me. The following are my questions and her grandmother's replies, written and translated by Xue Yan:

QUESTION: What do you remember about the period before 1949?

ANSWER: My grandma's life, like every average peasant at that period, can only be described as heart-rending. She had to spin for the rich men when she was still a child. Every time she returned home, her hands would be dotted with bubbles and her body sore from hair to the sole. She was born in 1931 and got married to my grandpa when she was eighteen and my grandpa fifteen. Grandma's family didn't own any land but served as the tenants for the rich landlords, who could get half of their harvests without any labor. However, my grandpa's family did have a paltry patch. Therefore, my grandparents had their own land to till. During the years 1945 to 1949, she only heard some gossip about the war between the KMT and the Red Army, but the war didn't disturb the tranquility of the small village by and large.

QUESTION: How did your life change after the Red Army arrived?

ANSWER: When the Red Army arrived, her life changed a lot. Before the army's arrival, however hard she toiled, she couldn't fill up her stomach, because she, together with her family, were exploited by the rich landlords for she only had a small morsel of land. After the Red Army's advent, she could have more to eat and didn't fear to starve. After the Red Army advocated a series of land reforms, the family got its own distribution of land (about one acre), which absolutely was a blessing for them. After she had the land, most of the time she worked alone, sometimes with her husband, but rarely with her neighbors, maybe because at that time, the commune hadn't come into existence. The rich landlords dispersed from the village but she didn't know where they fled.

QUESTION: Please describe your life during the 1950s.

ANSWER: She remembered three grand issues about the 1950s: the Great Leap Forward, the Korean War and the big famine in 1959. She didn't fight in the Korean War, which was too distant a thing for her. Life was manifestly better than before Liberation. For one thing, she and her children were warmly, though not decently, clothed and enough, though not lavishly, fed. For another, poor peasants were not looked down upon and they became the hosts of the society. She often says to me that the soldiers of the KMT Army tended to punch people to their hearts' content. However, the Red Army were lenient and sympathetic to the poor.

In the Great Leap Forward, the Fuyang local government bragged about the harvest and the bounty of its districts and meanwhile it carried out several grand projects, among which digging a gigantic river was an important one. My grandma carried her first son, my father, to join in this grand project, and she labored far away from her house altogether for three months. In the daytime, she shouldered the hoe to the designated place and set out to dig the river, leaving her child in a tent. At night, she slept with other female co-laborers in a tremendous tent, and another tent of the same size was intended for the men. Therefore, she didn't make steel but instead dug the river.

The wide-scale famine in 1959 was ingrained in my grandma's mind, and it was a horrible nightmare to her, for one of her children didn't survive that famine. After having eaten all the edible things in the house and even the edible grass and the barks of trees, my grandparents, with their children, set out to another county which was north of Funan county (Yingshang county) for survival. On the way to it, they begged and tried to exchange scanty food with hard labor for others. In spite of all this, the couple lost one of their beloved children, who was physically weaker than the others.

QUESTION: During the 1960s were you in a commune?

ANSWER: Even before the 1960s, my grandparents were in the commune, and they joined the senior commune in the village in the 1960s. At that time, all the peasants, whether aged or young, would share every meal cooked in a gigantic iron cauldron. Grandma did field work with the villager's women, and the work ranged from picking the cotton to wiping out the weeds. Out of respect to this institution, grandma nicknamed my father "*She Men*" (commune's gate).

QUESTION: What do you recall about the period of the Cultural Revolution from 1966–1976?

ANSWER: She remembers that the peasants in the village, at times, were called out to join meetings, during which Chairman Mao's speeches, poems and works were read. My grandma, together with the other villagers were required to recite them, although most of them were illiterate. Because such meetings were always dull and long-winded, grandma would prefer to sit at the back dozing. Grandma's children didn't study any more in the school. Instead, they ran hither and thither and played wildly like unyoked horses. Sometimes, they were lined up to parade in the main street and yelled something they didn't even understand.

QUESTION: What do you think of Mao Zedong?

ANSWER: To my grandma, Chairman Mao is both mysterious and sacred. She stolidly believes that without Chairman Mao, she wouldn't be warmly dressed and well-fed. In her opinion, Chairman Mao is for the poor peasants what the sun is for the dreadful darkness. She has been to Beijing once and there she bought a statue of Mao. When she came back, she put the statue on the long table in the sitting room side by side with the statue of the Mercy Goddess. After Chairman Mao passed away, he became something of a God. At every Chinese traditional festival, grandma will offer fruits before these statues, light several sticks of incense in the urn, kneel down and mutter some auspicious promises for the whole family.

QUESTION: What do you think about religion and did the Communist Party of China try to stop you from practicing your religion?

ANSWER: Among many Buddhist gods, she firmly believes in the Goddess of Mercy, because she thinks the Goddess is kind-hearted, sympathetic and helpful. Whenever she meets troubles or bad things, she can resort to the Goddess who is kind enough to help her out. Moreover, she believes good deeds can beget good results, because the Goddess is up there, watching us, guiding us to do good and blessing us for what we have done.

3

An Xin, Born in the 1980s

An Xin (pronounced shin) is the oldest student I interviewed and the one whose life story I got to know most fully. She introduced herself as my graduate teaching assistant on my first day of teaching, and a year later, when I left China, I waved good-bye to a young Chinese woman whose life had become intertwined with mine. She had been my personal assistant, tourist guide, interpreter, substitute teacher, and family friend. I had been a thesis adviser, personal confidante, guide to Western culture, and a second mother to her. Together we explored Hangzhou, toured Beijing, traveled to her hometown and to Xi'an in Shaanxi province, and celebrated the Chinese New Year. An Xin is forthright, undaunted by obstacles, assertive, and amazingly able to get things done. She is petite and pretty.

Because An Xin was a second-year graduate student, her story has more dimensions than the others and therefore merits its own chapter. After she completed her course work at Zhejiang University, she moved to Beijing in fall 2005 to begin full-time employment while at the same time writing a dissertation for a master's degree. She returned to Hangzhou three times before graduating in March 2006.

Childhood in Xianyang

An Xin is a northerner, an aspect of her background that remained significant for her while living in Hangzhou as a graduate student. According to tradition, southerners, whose diet is based on rice, are delicate and pacific, in contrast to northerners, who are wheat eaters and are robust and aggressive. She was born on July 5, 1981, in Xianyang in Shaanxi province, a city one hour west of Xi'an, which was China's ancient capital and is famed today for the exhibition of the life-sized Terracotta Army from Emperor Qinshihuang's tomb of the third century B.C.

Bounded on the east by the Yellow River and on the west by northwest China, the whole of Shaanxi province is rich in historical and cultural relics that encompass everything from Neolithic sites, imperial tombs, and palaces, to memorials of the Communist Revolution. It was in Yan'an in the northern reaches of the province where remnants of the Red Army (soldiers who had survived the 5000-mile Long March of 1934 to 1935) created the beginnings of a communist society. Israel Epstein, an European expatriate writer who made China his home, named the mountainous cave dwellings that housed Mao Zedong and the government in preparation during the 1930s as the "embryo of New China."

An Xin's family has deep roots in Xianyang, and the modest house in which she and her older brother grew up is just down the street from her mother's family dwelling. When her mother was a child, this city neighborhood was not urban at all, and An Xin refers to her mother's family as peasants. Today, uncles and cousins still live nearby within the small city of 400,000.

Her father's family originated in the surrounding countryside, but from the date of his birth in 1948, his landowning family experienced downward-spiraling fortunes blamed on his father's (An Xin's grandfather) addiction to opium. This grandfather died when An Xin was six years old, and she retains an image of sitting on his lap and feeling his bristling mustache rubbing against her cheeks.

I visited the second house that An Xin's parents had built during her childhood. They moved into this two-story building in the mid–1990s, but the city government expropriated it in 2004 as part of a planned facelifting of the neighborhood. It had not yet been torn down in summer 2005, so that I was able to walk into An Xin's former bedroom on the second floor from which she had looked out over neighboring buildings and clotheslines and where she had daydreamed about the future. I also saw the downstairs room, the site of her parents' continuous mahjong games and where An Xin had founded a children's English summer school during her vacations from university. The house was not large by any means, but when she was a child they had rented out one of the rooms to another family.

The family is very disgruntled about their house expropriation and have protested vehemently to officials at all levels of government: to the city of Xianyang, to the province of Shaanxi in Xi'an, and to the national government in Beijing. The protests were to no avail, and so

An Xin traveling home by train © 2005 (courtesy Christophe Agou).

her parents and brother, who works as a security guard at the city park, have moved into a two-bedroom apartment nearby, which they rent for $165 a month. The government has informed them that after the renovation has been completed, they will be able to move back.

They had lived in another house in the same neighborhood until her father had suffered an injury at work. This event had been a turning point for An Xin's family, for her father, a construction worker who had been the main breadwinner, was forced to retire after this accident. At the time, when An Xin was fourteen, she went to live with her maternal grandmother and entered the same junior middle school that her mother had attended.

Her older brother, who was born in 1979, shares none of her personal qualities, and their differences have created antipathy toward one another. In contrast to her, he dropped out of school and spent three years serving in the army. An Xin remembers her brother as a brutal sibling who used to beat her up. Now he works as a night guard in

Xianyang but is unable to earn enough money to live independently from his parents.

In all the time I knew her, An Xin's father was never as major a topic of conversation between us as was her mother. He had curtailed his schooling prematurely. As the eldest child, he had assumed familial responsibilities at a young age because of his father's opium addiction-related incapacitation. An Xin mentioned that he had taken care of his mother, who had died in the 1970s, before her parents married in 1977. He also had served in the army for three years, a voluntary decision, for there is no compulsory military service in China. The most surprising characteristic of her father is that he is the cook in the family, and her mother does the food shopping. When we prepared special dumplings together in Hangzhou in celebration of the Lunar New Year, An Xin telephoned her father to ask for the recipe.

An Xin's mother, in contrast to her husband, is a feisty character with a dominating personality. When she visited Hangzhou for the first time, her favorite activity was strolling around West Lake unguided by An Xin,

An Xin with her parents.

and she insisted that we accept as presents two huge bags of dates and walnuts that she had carried on the train from Xianyang. She was born in 1950 in Xianyang as one of six children to parents who were farmers of grain and corn. Her birth coincided with that of the People's Republic of China, and her life story shares many similarities with her country's: full of ups and downs. As a student in the early 1960s she learned Russian at middle school and worked on a commune from 1965 to 1976, where she was a women's brigade leader. One of the first things An Xin mentioned about her mother was that she had been a Red Guard, had traveled around China by train for free in 1966, and had seen Mao Zedong at a rally. Sure enough, when I looked through old photo albums of her family there was one of her mother in a Red Guard uniform.

"What happened then? Is she still a communist?" I asked An Xin. Her answer: "She fits her life into the currents of the times. During the 1980s she started a private clothing retail business with one of her four brothers." At first they sold men's suits, but they switched to shirts and trousers for young people as fashion demands shifted. When we stepped into *Liuxingqianxian*, which is the name of the family business, a sister-in-law greeted us and told us how she had tried to expand their business to Botswana in Africa, where her sister has operated a traditional Chinese medicine hospital for ten years. But the difficulties she encountered in attempting to sell clothing to Botswana overwhelmed her. In addition to language problems, she had trouble exchanging Chinese currency.

The retail business still functions in Xianyang, but An Xin's mother retired from it ten years ago when the daily routine became too strenuous. As a saleswoman she was standing up at the shop for long hours every day, traveling around China to buy wholesale goods, and riding a bicycle to the market stall where they sold the clothing. Her health suffered as a result, and in addition her husband suffered a stroke in 2003. During the past few years, she and her husband have operated a mahjong club in their house, but now she wants to begin learning English. When I met her parents for the first time during their trip to Hangzhou, her mother tried to say a few words in English but we both reverted to singing songs; she in Chinese and I in English while our husbands remained speechless.

An Xin's maternal grandparents had also changed their occupation from farmers to small businessmen when the Chinese economy opened up in 1979. They started a food business, cooking a popular breakfast food called *jing gao*, a combination of rice and dates, which they sold to customers in their own neighborhood. Her grandmother, who died at age 79 when An Xin was an undergraduate at university, had bound feet and yet had worked in both the fields and the house all her life.

The city of Xianyang has transformed itself from village to town to city in An Xin's lifetime. The airport that serves Xi'an is situated in Xianyang, which is only twenty-five miles away. As a sign of opening up the local economy in the early 1980s, Xianyang established an extensive outdoor and indoor marketplace, the site of her family's clothing shop, and constructed a sprawling industrial zone, where her wealthiest uncle operates a construction-materials company.

The city park and nearby restaurant, where we ate traditional lamb soup into which we tossed pieces of bread that we each crumbled up, were established during her mother's childhood in the 1950s. When An Xin was a child she would climb over the fence to the park to avoid paying the entrance fee that she could not afford. On the occasion of our visit we each paid the one *kuai* fee (about 13 cents), and her mother paid the equivalent of $3.50 to rent a pedalo boat. She insisted on taking command of the rudder and navigating us around the willow-lined lake. We peddled past the roller-skating rink, a large sculpture of a spotted tiger, billiard tables, children's amusements, and many snack stands, as her mother maneuvered our boat around fishing lines and lotus plants in flower.

In Xianyang's central square families gather outside on hot summer evenings and teenagers flock to the disco below ground, and we watched a group of elderly women bang on drums and perform dances while waving red cloths. Across the main street from this city plaza lies a modern shopping mall featuring McDonald's and an outdoor movie screen.

The Weihe River flows through Xianyang, and the new mayor has poured funds into development of a riverside walk and park. An Xin told me that her mother was pleased with the improvements. She, on the other hand, considered it irresponsible for the city to divert attention and resources away from solving the serious river pollution caused from an oil refinery and the dumping of untreated waste.

A large modern bridge crosses the river leading to Xi'an, where An Xin did her undergraduate studies. This well-preserved provincial capital has become one of China's major tourist destinations. Although the city is no longer the centerpiece of an imperial dynasty, a visitor today is still conscious of its importance in political, military, economic, and even religious Chinese history. Remains of the ancient fortifications still stand in the center of the city. Xi'an served as the capital of the Chinese Confucian empire for more than a thousand years, reaching its peak during the Tang dynasty (618 to 907 A.D.) when the city was called Chang'an and was home to two million Chinese. To honor their history and enhance tourism many modern Chinese cities have decided to highlight their connections with ancient civilizations. Hangzhou, for instance, is associated with the Song dynasty, and the Forbidden City in Beijing with the Ming dynasty. Accordingly, Xi'an has constructed a Tang dynasty street.

In addition to exhibitions of imperial grandeur, twentieth-first-century Xi'an, with its 3.6 million inhabitants, reflects its cosmopolitan past and its situation as a gateway to northwest China. If you enter the old town through the city wall on the south and walk underneath the Drum Tower, passing by McDonald's, you will find yourself on an ethnic Moslem street. Here, restaurants serving dishes such as hot pots and lamb skewers prevail, and around the corner lie the gardens and gilded wooden Koran of the Great Mosque, built in 742, with its distinctive blend of Chinese and Arabic landscape and architectural design. This quarter evokes historical images of the days when Arab and Persian merchants settled in Xi'an to be well-positioned at the start of the Silk Road. As early as 138 B.C. caravans of camels plied their trade between China, India, central Asia, the Middle East, and countries of the Mediterranean. Transporting goods via the Silk Road dominated East/West trade and communication until the fourteenth century or so, when shipping lanes began to displace the overland routes. Within the modern city of Xi'an, with cultural links to this historical era, an ethnic minority community of approximately 60,000 Moslem Hui still resides.

Not only does present-day Xi'an abound in Confucian and Islamic cultural relics, but vivid reminders of its Chinese Buddhist heritage are also much in evidence. The connection between Buddhism and Xi'an is given short shrift and is even overlooked by tourists overwhelmed at the site of Emperor Qin's 7000 terracotta warriors. Yet, from the fifth to eighth centuries and especially during the reign of Empress Wu (683 to 705), Chang'an (i.e., Xi'an) was the capital of Buddhist China. In 652 A.D. the entire city welcomed home pilgrim Xuan Zang, who after studying Buddhism in India for eighteen years then devoted the rest of his life to translating Buddhist texts into Chinese. One of the most popular traditional Chinese stories, *Journey to the West* (sometimes also called *The Monkey King*), is based on Xuan Zang's travels. In 2006 two Chinese Buddhist monks retraced his journey, departing from Xi'an and following his exact route to India. Also located in Xi'an are the two Wild-Goose pagodas, which were built during the Tang dynasty. They house important Buddhist texts and impressive artifacts and carvings. In nearby Fufeng County, the remains of what are said to be Buddha's fingers have been discovered at the Famen Temple.

Even though An Xin did not move to Xi'an until she completed high school, still she had been exposed to big city life earlier than many other Chinese university students. Before her father's accident, the family had made the fourteen-hour train journey to Beijing, where she had her photograph taken in Tian'anmen Square and joined the queue through Mao Zedong's mausoleum. During her childhood in Xianyang, she had visited some of the historical landmarks in Xi'an but not the prime archaeological site, the Terracotta Army, even though this world-renowned find had been discovered accidentally by peasants digging a well in 1974, several years before her birth.

An Xin cherishes her memories of childhood, and in *China Youth* magazine in October 2005 she wrote about her nostalgia for those comparatively carefree times. In her article she draws a sharp contrast between her youth and the future she imagines: a period filled with concerns about earning a living, anxieties about her parents' welfare, and problems associated with living in a complicated world.

University in Xi'an

An Xin remained in Xianyang and did not board away from home during middle school or high school, but after passing the college-entrance examination she chose to study English at Xi'an Foreign Languages University (now renamed Xi'an International Studies University). This university, situated in the southern district of the city outside the city walls, was founded in 1952 and at first focused on the study of Russian. By the time An Xin began her studies in 1999 the university offered programs in eight foreign languages: English, Russian, Japanese, German, French, Spanish, Italian, and Korean. As if to highlight its distinctive international slant, the university has erected on the lawn behind the administration building statues of the leading authors from many of the world's literatures: Goethe, Shakespeare, Dante, Cervantes, Victor Hugo, Pushkin, and China's early twentieth-century writer Lu Xun. China has established only eight foreign-language universities, all of which are located in places where international relations are central: Beijing, Shanghai, Guangzhou, Dalian, Tianjin, Chongqing, Luoyang, and Xi'an.

Because in China the study of foreign languages is dominated by women, the vast majority of the 12,000 students at An Xin's alma mater are female. In fact, when I entered the compact and neatly landscaped campus, it gave the appearance of a women's college in the United States. The scale was small in comparison with Zhejiang University and the dormitories fronted onto the outdoor playing fields. While a student there An Xin played on the soccer team and also participated in theatrical productions, acting the role of the youngest daughter in *The Sound of Music*. She still keeps intact a positive image of her four years as an undergraduate and returns to the campus every time she visits her family in Xianyang — but not for long, for as happens with most higher-education institutions in China, this university is relocating to the city's suburbs beginning in the fall semester of 2005.

An Xin appreciated the education that she received at this university, especially the opportunity to meet American and British visiting professors, but realized the limitations of an academic approach that emphasized primarily the study of language. As her fluency in spoken and written English improved, her enthusiasm and interest in English literature increased. Because of her limited exposure to literature during her course of study as an undergraduate she decided to continue studying English literature in graduate school.

One of her undergraduate roommates, also an English major whom I met during my visit, had chosen another track and had moved directly into the working world in 2003 after graduation from Xi'an International Studies University. Her job as a foreign affairs officer at the Chinese Space Agency in Xi'an seemed enviable. Yet, she told us that in fact she makes little use of her English studies: "The foreigners we interact with in the space program are mainly Russians and Turks, and they do not communicate in English."

An Xin also had considered an alternative path after finishing her undergraduate education. She had traveled to Guilin in southwest Guanxi province, home to a renowned scenic landscape of strangely-shaped limestone peaks, where she had begun training to become a tourist guide. In the end, the opportunity to study for a master's degree at Zhejiang University appealed to her more. However, when in Guilin, she met a young photographer who worked for a photography magazine in Beijing. Their initial encounter marked the start of a three-year romance, and the beginning of frequent triangular travel between Hangzhou, Beijing, and Guilin.

Two other college roommates with whom she had remained in contact also continued onto graduate school directly after receiving their bachelor's degrees. One studied law at Peking University and afterwards returned to work in Xi'an and another remained at Xi'an International Studies University. An Xin recently reunited with her on the Tsinghua University campus in Beijing, where she works and where her former roommate was taking the entrance examination for doctoral studies.

Graduate School in Hangzhou

After I had known An Xin for a few months, I asked her why she had chosen Zhejiang University for graduate school. Her reply took me by surprise: "It appealed to me because one of my favorite writers, Mr. Louis Cha (pen name Jin Yong), was associated with this university." This answer astonished me because of what it revealed about her taste in literature. Jin Yong is a popular writer, famous for martial arts novels that were published originally as installments in Hong Kong newspapers where he worked. In contrast, she also counted British Victorian author George Eliot as one of her favorites. Wide-ranging taste, so it would seem.

A lot about An Xin surprised me. She was her own person: eager to experience life, able, opinionated, and conscious of being a woman. Once our relationship of professor and assistant had been solidified after she had xeroxed mountains of readings for my graduate English literature class, we moved on to more enjoyable shared activities, such as visiting libraries and museums and sightseeing in Hangzhou. Because An Xin had moved to this city only one year earlier, she had not yet explored all its places of interest.

One of our first excursions together was an afternoon outing to the Six Harmonies Pagoda, which is situated in the south of Hangzhou overlooking the Qiantang River. We decided to travel there by school bus, taking advantage of a scheduled shuttle service that assists teachers and students to participate in courses at any one of the six campuses of Zhejiang University. I used one of these buses to commute between the campus where I lived and the campus where I taught. The pagoda lies adjacent to Zhijiang campus, one of the six campuses of Zhejiang University, so we would save on transportation expenses by taking the school bus. I was conscious always of the huge disparity in our incomes, with An Xin earning 500 *yuan* ($63) a month in comparison with my 6,000 *yuan* ($750) a month, and yet she balked at my paying for our taxi rides together.

We also decided that we would stroll around Zhijiang campus before touring the pagoda. I had read that this campus originally had been an American Christian college founded in 1845 by an American doctor. It had been managed by the Chinese Christian Association, but its main source of funds had come from the United States. In 1952 the Chinese government took over all private colleges, and this educational facility continued to function as one of Hangzhou's institutions of higher education. This background information was especially interesting to An Xin, who has never traveled abroad but has tried to understand English literature with its abundance of Christian references and underlying cultural context. The architecture of the campus was distinctively non–Chinese; the brick buildings were laid out in quadrangles with formal British-style gardens. She took a photograph of a three-story structure with a clock tower that told the time in Roman numerals. We even spotted a stone church that had been shuttered but was left still standing and undamaged. However, reading the names of the trees was of little use to me, for they were identified and labeled in Latin and Chinese only.

An Xin had known about the existence of this campus, as one of her roommates who taught an English class there had told her how far away it was from the Zijingang campus, where their dorms were located. But she was surprised and excited by the cultural differences she observed in the setting and architecture at Zhijiang. An Xin also was employed as a part-time English teacher at Shu Ren private university in the northeast district of Hangzhou. Private universities exist in China, but they are not central to the system of higher education, and up to now have tended to attract academically weak students. Her teaching experience at Shu Ren was so discouraging for her, with the students uninterested in the subject matter and impossible to engage in discussion, that it had dissuaded her from pursuing a future career in teaching.

We walked away from Zhijiang campus toward the Pagoda of Six Harmonies, which is situated above the Qiantang River. From the top of the pagoda, we enjoyed splendid views of the green hills of the southern section of the city, of the bridges and river barges, and of the new architecture of expanding Hangzhou on the other bank. What appealed to An Xin most was the sight of the forested hills, and she told me that, only a few weeks before, she had hiked several miles along those ridges together with 5000 other students on an outing organized by the university.

The Buddhist pagoda, although a tourist site today, was constructed initially in the tenth century as a monument to the gods, as a plea for calmer tides on the Qiantang River. Because of a tidal bore in the Gulf of Hangzhou at the mouth of the river, every year surging tides occur, sometimes as high as thirty feet, which are both spectacular to behold and infamous for the havoc they wreak.

After climbing up and down all seven floors to the top of the pagoda, we rested in the park at the base and chatted. She told me that she was beginning to formulate the specific topic for her master's dissertation on George Eliot. She knew that she wanted to analyze Eliot's female characters and was intrigued by the paradox between the conventional fictional lives that Eliot wrote about and the liberated life that the authoress had lived.

An Xin then brought the conversation back to her own life with her boyfriend, who was in Beijing working as an editor on a photography magazine. This boyfriend did not support her ambition, but was trying to persuade her to move to Beijing to find a well-paid job so that he could pursue his dream of becoming a full-time photographer. "He isn't interested in my studies at all," she said, "and yet I encourage him in his photography." She kept finding parallels between herself and George Eliot, who had found happiness and male support only in a twenty-year illegitimate marriage. An Xin also complained about her boyfriend's continual purchase of new cameras. "He doesn't even think about the expense," she bemoaned; but she had already figured out for herself the root cause for their conflict about money: "He comes from a more privileged family than mine; his father works for the government in Guilin, his mother teaches music at a middle school, and his grandfather was a renowned artist."

94

"But what do you want to do with your life?" I asked An Xin. She was not sure but had always thought that she would help Chinese people who were less fortunate than she. At that time she had just applied to work in a special program in Guizhou province, a poor region in southwest China. There in the city of Zunyi, Zhejiang University was planning to send young graduate students to teach English in middle schools.

This program appealed to her on several counts. Zunyi had played a historic role for Zhejiang University, as it was the site where the university had been based from 1938 to 1946. When Japanese troops occupied Hangzhou in 1937, professors and students packed up their books, laboratories, and classrooms and started out on a long march to find a new home for the university. After marching for more than one year on a trek that included stops at monasteries and schools to hold classes for a few months at a stretch, the university set up a campus in exile in the city of Zunyi, approximately 1000 miles to the west of Hangzhou. Now in 2005 Zhejiang University in Hangzhou is thriving, and the city (and province) where it is situated is considered to be one of the most prosperous areas of China. However, just the opposite could be said about Zunyi, and a number of projects have been proposed to reverse the fortunes of Zunyi as a means of thanking the city for the hospitality it displayed toward Zhejiang University during its time of need.

An Xin had applied to participate in this program for a personal reason as well. Before she had left home to begin university in Xi'an, she and her mother had discussed her future ambition to teach school in a poor region of China. Her mother had advised her against this plan, hoping that her daughter's career could become more remunerative. An Xin's altruistic ideal had never vanished completely from her mind, and applying to this program had reignited the dream. In the end, the program failed to materialize because there were not enough applicants, not enough graduate students like An Xin at Zhejiang University. She, on the other hand, did not entirely abandon this cause, for she has contributed funds out of her meager earnings from her various part-time jobs to pay the school fees for a child in Yunnan province.

Not only was An Xin an assistant and companion to me, but she also befriended my husband. Among the excursions in and around Hangzhou that we undertook with An Xin, our trip to the Meijiawu tea culture village in the southwestern outskirts of the city was one of the most successful. We boarded a city bus, in which residents immediately stood up so that we elderly foreigners could sit down. But this time we were not the only tourists. We conversed in English with an accountant from Shanghai who was on an all-day excursion with her parents, having just returned from Houston, Texas, where she had worked for several years. We also talked with a young man from Nigeria who spoke fluent Chinese, which he had acquired after only two years living in China as a teacher of English.

When we arrived in the village, the hills were alive with tea buds but we discovered that the end of March was a few weeks too early for this year's harvest of Dragon Well tea. We strolled through the village with its curious mixture of modern restaurants next to women washing clothes in the stream until we came to the memorial to Zhou Enlai. The former Chinese prime minister, who died in 1976, had visited workers in this village five times and on one occasion had brought along the President of Ceylon (now known as Sri Lanka). When we visited the fields of tea, An Xin had asked several village women how much money they earned; their answer, $3 a day for picking tea from 6:00 A.M. to 6:00 P.M. In the 1950s, when Zhou Enlai visited, their labor was organized and remunerated collectively through their workers' brigade.

Touring this memorial with An Xin made me curious about her opinions about Chinese Communist history. In accordance with many university students who were born in the 1980s, An Xin is a member of the Communist Party. She was recommended by party members at the university, went through an inauguration ceremony, and attends periodic meetings. In contrast to many other Communist students, however, she is not dismissive of the political education taught to her since middle school. She spoke favorably even about the political courses that she was required to take while studying English literature in graduate school. Yet, she insisted that politics did not interest her, although she was very concerned about the severe social problems that China faces and wanted to continue voicing her own opinions. She often became exercised when discussing the hypocrisy and favoritism shown by leaders at all levels of society, whether at university, in business, or in government.

Another graduate student who belonged to the Party said that she believed in the reformed communist ideology of "creating a socialist society with Chinese characteristics." Yet, as a student of economics, this young woman assumed that Communist Party membership would assist her job search in a multinational company. Other pragmatic students concurred with these notions, usually admitting that they had joined the Party because it represented the establishment, and in the hope that networking among Party members could advance their career prospects.

Working Life

Even before An Xin finished writing her master's dissertation on the anxieties of the female characters in George Eliot's *Daniel Deronda*, she decided to leave Hangzhou in order to find a job in Beijing. The allure of working in the capital city is strong for recent university graduates in China today, but in An Xin's case it was not the attraction to Beijing but rather to her boyfriend that moved her there.

She followed no blueprint for entering this next stage of life, but several steps seemed familiar, similar to the ways that any young graduate anywhere in the world would proceed. Her first idea for employment, a type of job that she thought would make use of her education, was to work as an editor or translator for a publisher. She assembled a resume, which she printed out in both English and Chinese, and asked her boyfriend to circulate it to his contacts and friends at publishing companies. For a few weeks she sat in her boyfriend's gloomy basement apartment waiting for the phone to ring, inviting her for an interview. That did not happen, so she ventured out in another direction.

She surfed the Internet, focusing on publishers' Websites that advertised job openings. She found one at a weekly English-language newspaper called *Student Times* whose audience is middle-school students. This publisher gave her a job as an editor. During the three weeks that she worked there her assignment was to edit examination questions and answers that tested English vocabulary, grammar, and word patterns. She did not leave her first job out of dissatisfaction; on the contrary, she had found her colleagues friendly and willing to help her to adjust to the work environment. She left because she was recruited by another publishing company and promised a higher salary.

That was not all; there was another twist to her employment saga. The day before she was to leave *Student Times*, she was interviewed by the Department of Environmental Sciences and Engineering at Tsinghua

University for a position as English interpreter and external-affairs officer. A colleague had recommended her, and she could not resist the temptation to work at China's leading university. She was offered this job, too, but she had already agreed to start work at the publishing company as a translator from English into Chinese of books for young children. In the end, she was employed for only one week at this company, which afterwards gave her another translation assignment on a free-lance basis.

In November An Xin began her third job in Beijing, as an external-affairs officer at Tsinghua University. In the meantime, however, she and her boyfriend had broken up and she needed to find a roommate and an apartment. Again she turned to the Internet, this time placing two personal ads at Websites for roommates, one in English and one in Chinese. Through this search, she met Mary, a young woman from England who spoke Chinese and was employed at a hospital in Beijing. Together they looked for an apartment to rent and found one in the northern district of the city, near the Summer Palace.

After borrowing money from her parents to pay her share of the required three months' rent in advance, they moved into a furnished one-bedroom flat that belongs to an employee at the nearby agricultural institute. The location is convenient for An Xin's job at Tsinghua University; she commutes by bus for twenty minutes and then transfers to a bicycle that she leaves at the entrance to the campus. However, the apartment is not convenient to downtown Beijing, which is two hours away by public transportation.

Her responsibilities at this job combine administrative tasks dealing with visiting foreign scholars and English interpretation in the field of environmental science. To become conversant in this subject, which was quite new to her, she has taken environmental-policy classes at the university. Her first assignment was to write a brochure in both English and Chinese about the Department of Environmental Sciences and Engineering. When it was completed several months later, An Xin sent us a copy of the 12-page color booklet. "It felt like a child of mine. I participated in the whole process from material collecting in the very beginning, to the designing, and then paying the printing company," she added in an accompanying note.

During her first year at this job she accumulated a wide range of experiences in program management. The climactic event took place in

October 2006 when she managed the organization of an UNESCO work-shop entitled "Engineering Education for Sustainable Development," hosted by her university department. Tsinghua University professor Qian Yi initiated the two-day meeting, which involved both plenary and small-group sessions and included twenty-five international participants from Nigeria, Thailand, India, the Philippines, Bahrain, and Pakistan, among other countries.

She found the working experience "much more rewarding" than she had expected. In an email soon after the workshop ended, she wrote:

> I was the main contact with foreign participants regarding their travel arrangements. I made the task list for my colleagues as well as for students from my department who worked on the workshop and interacted with people from other departments of the university who helped with the organization of the five parallel sessions. I also was in charge of writing the guidebook for the workshop.
>
> What delighted me beside the appreciation from the participants is that I built a working team with lots of cooperative members, especially the students. Some of them are really helpful and responsible, and they reminded me of details that I hadn't paid attention to. They undertook my task when I was tired and they didn't complain when I acted like an unreasonable boss. They gave me support, courage and confidence.

After excitedly describing the success of this event, she ended her email message with a reference to her mother: "I guess I inherited the talent in management from my Mum.... She has always wanted to be the boss and I am sure if she were born in my time and had the chance to go to universities like I did she would have been an excellent manager or CEO. You know, she is much more talented than I am." From what I learned about An Xin's attributes, this comparison with her mother seems a bit disingenuous. It was An Xin who managed to resolve every problem and to arrange every excursion for us with an efficiency that we marveled at.

This job at Tsinghua University has brought other benefits for An Xin as well. At the end of the year, she sang in the chorus at the university's famous concert hall, an experience she found "very pleasant, so I kept smiling while singing." And then there was an organized staff excursion to Tianjin, a port city only an hour away from Beijing. That was not as pleasant for her, for "all we did there was shop and I really don't find shopping interesting."

In May 2006, as yet another bonus to this job, she accompanied an official delegation of Chinese mayors as an assistant and an interpreter on an environmental study tour to the United States, a trip that included stops in New York City, Yale University, Chicago, Milwaukee, Portland, Oregon, and San Francisco. When she returned to Beijing, she wrote to me about her reactions:

> It was weird because while I was in San Francisco, the last stop of our trip, I missed China so much that I wanted to fly back instantly. While I am here back in China, I miss my life in the States. Yes, I do miss the comfort of life in your country, hotels with shower, iron and hairdryer, so that I don't have to wait for one hour for the heating in my bathroom to begin to work, don't have to bring my suit to the laundry and go to bed with my hair wet. I began to understand why so many Mexicans (of course not only Mexicans) tried hard to cross the border to be in America. While we were in the States, we often complained that you Americans live such an extravagant life. But I think somehow every one of us wants to live this life deep in our heart. We just don't have the choice.
>
> You know what is the first thing that struck me in America? It's the cut-through between black and white. When I walked out of the plane in JFK, all of the people waiting outside to clean the plane were black. All the men carrying luggage were black. But the people who sat behind the desk to check our documents were white. Remember I told you I once took the wrong bus and kind of got lost? It happened while we were at Yale, the most beautiful place I could ever imagine. The bus actually took me to an adjacent town which is called West Haven. The warm-hearted bus driver, who comforted me when I found that I had taken the wrong bus, was black and almost 90 percent of her passengers were black. The only white passenger I remember is a man who I think is too fat to work. It seemed the whole town was taken up by black. I saw a black little girl sitting outside the porch of her house and black boys hanging out idly. The bus also stopped at a quite large health care center, and before it actually left New Haven, I saw a sign on a street which said "drug-free" area. Later I was told that district is also taken by blacks.
>
> All our way from New York to Chicago, I saw most of the service jobs were done by blacks until we got to San Francisco where the service jobs were taken over by Mexicans and Chinese. I just read Amy Tan's *Joy Luck Club* and *The Color Purple* by Alice Walker. They reminded me of the scenes that I saw in the States. I can't help

100

asking: Can they really melt into one country or one consciousness, be it Black, Yellow, or Caucasian? What do you think?

It's hard to summarize my reaction towards America. I can't deny what I saw. I would say America is a very good country if there were no wars; if he could give up some of his wealth to make the world a better place.

This trip to the United States was not the first time that An Xin had acted as an interpreter. During summer 2005 at an international photography exhibition in Guilin, she had interpreted for both English and American photographers. She also coordinated at summer English camps, acting as an interpreter between foreign teachers and Chinese school administrators.

Her next steps in life are yet to be determined, for she says that she is still searching for what she really wants to do. Perhaps An Xin's decision-making is especially complicated because of her versatility. She is translating into Chinese the book *Moving Out*, essays about Swiss-American photographer Robert Frank, and had seriously considered studying for a doctorate degree in the theory of photography. At Zhejiang University she was good both as an administrative assistant and as a teaching assistant. She graded papers, took notes at meetings, wrote Chinese messages for me, and took over my American literature class when suddenly I had to leave China to visit my sick mother. Students appreciated her remarks about imagery in Nathaniel Hawthorne's story "Rappaccini's Daughter," and also her opinions, contrary to mine, about Arthur Miller's use of female characters in *All My Sons* and her interpretation of Ernest Hemingway's story "The Three-Day Blow." She was able to learn enough about Jewish culture to analyze the impact of patriarchal hierarchy on two Jewish female characters in George Eliot's *Daniel Deronda*. And yet she says that she doesn't want to become an English professor.

She criticized her classmates for being self-centered and competitive, perhaps because she was innately thoughtful of others. She was able to appreciate the talents of fellow students, praising Fan Gao's poetry and Xue Yan's ability to write essays. She bought my mother a hand-painted Hangzhou fan as a get-well present, even though she had no extra spending money. She spent days tracking down an address so that someone could receive a photograph in the mail.

She remains a young northern Chinese woman, more comfortable eating noodles than rice and more attuned to the boldness of Beijing than the dubious tact of Hangzhou. She misses the beauty of West Lake, but relishes the opportunities for living an eventful life in what she calls "the least beautiful city in China, Beijing."

An Xin's success in a challenging job at Tsinghua University has revealed her special talents: a sharp intelligence and ability to comprehend knowledge quickly combined with exceptional management skills. What's more, this job has awakened in her a passion and determination to work for a cause. In An Xin's words: "I have cultivated a strong interest in environmental and natural conservation issues in China and would like to devote myself to become part of the solution to the problems."

PART TWO: TEACHERS

The Chinese people in their thirties, forties and fifties whom I was most closely associated with during my year in China were my colleagues, other university professors. Mainly they were teachers in the English department at Zhejiang University, but I also met scientists and, in one instance, a young professor of English from another university in Hangzhou.

I have divided this part of the book into two chapters: the first focuses on teachers who were born in the 1970s and the second on older faculty who were born in the 1960s and 1950s. Naturally all three "generations" faced some similarities in their life experiences, but I was most impressed by the differences. During every historical decade since 1949 Chinese society has changed fundamentally, and those altered features of society have affected everyone's lives. The most striking break occurred after the death of Mao Zedong in 1976. Those born in the 1970s represent the post–Mao generation, while those born in the 1960s and 1950s experienced Mao's revolutionary policies.

Teachers who were born in the 1970s received their schooling in the era of China's opening up to the world. The subjects that they were taught as well as the lessons in morality and communism may not have changed significantly from earlier decades, but Chinese society beyond the school walls was undergoing radical transformation. When they reached maturity in the 1990s, they encountered a wide array of career choices and a variety of lifestyles.

In contrast, teachers who were born in the 1960s and 1950s were educated during a period of communist fervor amidst limited economic prosperity. They lived through the decade of the Cultural Revolution, although those born in the 1950s were more affected by those historical events than were the 1960s "generation."

The occupation of teacher is still appreciated in China today, reflected in the continuing celebration of Teachers' Day in September each year. In 2006, the daughter of a Beijing professor received a personal letter from President Hu Jintao at the time of her father's premature death at the age of 49. Hu wrote that, as he was a teacher of Chinese culture and literature, his death "is a great loss to the family, school and the country's educational undertaking" (*China Daily*, September 8, 2006). He encouraged the daughter to carry on her father's career, and China's minister of education viewed the letter "as an encouragement to teachers nationwide" (Ibid).

Several university students in my English writing classes wrote essays about teachers either as role models or as sources of inspiration. Invariably, the teachers they chose were born in the 1950s or 1960s and had succeeded in their profession because of their determination to fulfill their own aspirations. As one student put it: "The road of life is dotted with pebbles and boulders." She described her supervisor in biology, who "had spent a great amount of time and energy to become a scientist when there were inferior apparatus and deficient books.... In the peak of his career, however, when living and doing research in Japan and America, he abandoned those superior research resources and high salary to come back to China." She regards this man as "a precious example in both life and for work. To be perseverant and to get ready to devote myself to my country is inspiring whenever I feel tired and want to give up."

Another student wrote about her dad, who is a geography teacher in a rural school. She explained that because he was born in the 1950s he had been transferred to the countryside after finishing school. She wrote:

> There he led a simple life, according to him, working in the field during the day time and sleeping fast in the night. He told me that that kind of life was tranquil and peaceful, though tiring. Four or five years later, he became a geography teacher in a local school. At the same time, he got the opportunity to come back to the city and undertake a good job with high salary. However, my dad chose to stay in the countryside and teach those poor children.
> I was a frequent guest at that school when I was a child. I used to sit on the back of my dad's bicycle and be cycled there. The road was

so rugged and uneven that my back always hurt. However, the natural scenery alongside always refreshed me. The green fields of crops were paradise for butterflies. They danced and invited their close friends, dragonflies. Dragonflies asked orioles to play music for them....

I began to know why dad chose to stay. This is what one cannot find in a city. When getting to his school, dad pushed me encouragingly towards his students. At first, I felt a little sick at the boys with running noses and girls with tangled hair. Dad told me that "people in rags may have hearts of crystal. I should not judge people by their appearance." I played with them and shared my candies with them.

Dad is an excellent teacher. Without the textbook and notes, he can give a wonderful lesson and make everyone in the class understand clearly. He can draw the map of our country exactly. He said, "when one loves his job, he will do well in it."

Another student featured both her parents, who were schoolteachers, in her essay. However, she wrote that they did not advise her to follow in their footsteps:

It is strange that when I was very young and when I admired the career, they didn't encourage my dream. They told me that being a teacher, I had to work very hard and could only be paid a little.... At last, I respected my parents' wish and didn't choose to study at a teachers' college. But I know that wasn't because I didn't love it. Mother is tired and not paid much, but she is proud and happy for her occupation and her loving students.

4

Born in the 1970s

Chinese who were born in the 1970s are in a transitional group. They grew up during a period of frantic social and economic transformation with career options never before imaginable. Some have risen to millionaire status as CEOs or entrepreneurs in high-tech start-ups, taking risks and benefiting from the range of new opportunities in an economy opened up to the outside world. A few members of the "thirty-something" generation have made headlines for accumulating assets worth more than a billion dollars, while others have landed in prison for their excesses.

Teachers born in the 1970s, who are now adults immersed in their professional careers, are being asked to adjust to a continually changing educational environment. Trying to meet both career and societal challenges often means more studying, competing, and staying abreast of the latest developments. They may be second-rate calligraphers, but each is adept at cell-phone and computer-keyboard communication. The three teachers of English featured in this chapter have to balance their personal aspirations with the realities of contemporary China. All of them are living altogether differently from their parents in respect to educational level, career choice and advancement, housing and family circumstances.

The most junior faculty members in the English department at Zhejiang University were born in the 1970s and began their teaching careers after completing master's degrees. Most of these teachers have not studied abroad, and even though their subject is English, few have ever traveled to an English-speaking country. In order to continue in employment at the university, they now are required to pursue doctoral studies.

Until the late 1990s teachers did not need to compete in the job market to find employment. Their positions were assigned following graduation. Two of the teachers portrayed in this chapter fit into this category, but the youngest of the three was required to apply to several institutions and to interview to secure even a temporary teaching position.

Because they were born in the 1970s, before the introduction of China's one-child policy, they grew up in large families with several siblings. They attended primary school during the decade that followed the Cultural Revolution, so that many of the readings, textbooks, and moral teachings used in schools during the 1980s reflected ideas left over from Mao's China. Children were taught to emulate heroes. "Learn from Lei Feng, who was selfless and thoughtful, always ready to help others with good deeds," was a popular method for teaching good behavior (*A Nation at School*, Beijing Review Special Feature Series, 1983. p.104). A model student exemplified the "three goods: be good ideologically, study hard and keep physically fit" (Ibid).

Early education infused in this generation attitudes towards life in sharp contrast to the reformed attitudes that emerged during the post–1978 era of opening up to the outside world. Educators in the early 1980s still feared undue influence from "decadent thoughts and life styles" (*A Nation at School*, p. 109). As Shirley, one of the young teachers at Zhejiang University whom I interviewed, put it, "I feel a deep generation gap with my students," who were born only one decade later.

I interviewed two professors of English who were both born in Zhejiang province during the 1970s: one, whom I called Shirley, teaches at Zhejiang University; and the other, a male English teacher, whose name is Shao Bin, teaches at the Zhejiang University of Finance and Economics, one of several other government-operated institutions of higher education in Hangzhou. I also interviewed Alice, who teaches English at a senior middle school in southern Zhejiang province and whom I met during her leave of absence to study for a master's degree at Zhejiang University.

Shirley

I became well acquainted with several young English teachers at Zhejiang University, many of whom were young women trying to cope with child care alongside their heavy teaching, administration, and research schedules. These married teachers worked full-time, had begun doctoral programs at Zhejiang University, and had an additional extended family member residing in their apartments to help out in the household.

Although they always appeared to be frantically busy, balancing the various demands on their lives, nonetheless they seemed especially able to take advantage of the latest opportunities in Chinese society. Shirley, for instance, bought her two-year-old daughter a winter snowsuit over the Internet, and I often saw another young mother hurriedly parking her new car before rushing into class.

I had arranged to meet Shirley on a Friday afternoon at a time when there were no scheduled classes at Zhejiang University. She had agreed to accompany me on a visit to Hangzhou Middle School. One aspect of Chinese society that I had hoped to observe and understand during my year in China was school education. My interest in this area is particularly strong because previously I had written a history book about women public schoolteachers in the United States and had worked in Washington, D.C., at a nonprofit association whose purpose was to improve American school education.

Shirley's doctoral adviser, who is on the faculty at the university's department of education, had recommended her to be my guide. I realized, however, after I had gotten to know Shirley better that she was really too busy to appreciate having yet another assignment: me. Months after that first meeting she shared with me the story of her family, childhood, and career, and I was able to meet her two-year-old daughter, when I accompanied Shirley as she walked her bicycle to fetch her toddler from day care.

Childhood

Shirley was born in December 1973 in Shaoxing, a small city in Zhejiang province that is only 37 miles from Hangzhou. Zhejiang University attracts a large percentage of students from this famous cultural place, a

Shirley and daughter.

statistic I appreciated after reading thirty essays in response to my first writing assignment: "describe your hometown." Both of her parents, who were born in 1936, also came originally from this city known to tourists for its rice wine, houses built along canals, stone-arched bridges, and boats oared by foot.

Shaoxing is the hometown of a long list of celebrities, especially writers, artists, academics, and politicians. The city has chosen to highlight in particular Lu Xun (1881–1936), China's twentieth-century cultural icon, by demarcating an entire street and constructing a two-story museum devoted to his life and achievements. Although Lu Xun died before New China was born, his short stories, such as "The True Story of Ah Q" and "Diary of a Madman," have retained a cherished reputation and are known to every school child. He introduced into China the Western-style short story and criticized both traditional Confucian culture and the hypocrisy of upper-class intellectuals. During his last ten years of life in Shanghai he headed the League of Left-wing Writers. Beyond politics, however, he probed the Chinese psyche. His depiction of a humiliated, everyman character led to the coining of the term "Ah Quism," after his short story about Ah Q.

A thriving economy also has made headlines for Shaoxing. Residents credit the city's success to an early introduction of light industries, focused around textile production and markets. Prosperity has spread to outlying districts as well, where the creation of nonagricultural jobs for farmers and urbanization of rural areas have been priorities. Both Shirley's father and older brother were employed in the textile business at one time. Until 1997, when he retired at the age of sixty, her father had worked at a factory near to the house where she grew up. Her brother had started his working life at this same textile factory but had transferred, after his marriage, to a job at his wife's private publishing company, taking advantage of continually changing opportunities.

Even though Shirley's parents both grew up in the vicinity of Shaoxing, they did not meet one another there. In fact, their marriage is related to an important chapter in the history of Zhejiang province: the construction of the Xin'an River hydroelectric power station and creation of a huge man-made reservoir called the Thousand Island Lake. This construction project was one of the first to be undertaken after the founding of the People's Republic of China in 1949. The reservoir was completed in 1959 and the first of the power stations was activated in the early 1960s.

When Shirley's mother was twenty years old in 1956, instead of moving with the rest of her family to Hangzhou, she chose to venture off to the western region of the province to work as a cook at the massive dam site. Shirley's father was there also, employed as a construction worker. After their marriage they returned to Shaoxing and moved into a two-family house situated along one of the many waterways that wind through the city. They started a family and had three children: her brother, who was born in the early 1960s; her sister, who is ten years her senior, and the youngest child, Shirley, who was born in the early 1970s.

Education

The primary school she attended was near to her family's house and to the textile factory where her father worked, as was her junior middle school where she began learning English. It was not until Shirley went off to senior middle school that she became academically inclined and directed toward acquiring a university education. Although she had always excelled at school, she had not intended to continue her education beyond the requisite nine years.

As she explained to me, "I was raised under the red flag, believing in communist ideals." In the early 1980s, even though basic academic subjects, especially Chinese and mathematics, were strongly emphasized, primary-school students were required to take one class per week of manual labor. Fourth- and fifth-grade students participated in activities organized by their schools, such as planting trees, cleaning public places, and in some places operating small factories. Besides her studies, she had always been attracted to handwork, especially sewing and knitting, and had imagined herself entering the textile business one day.

But in senior middle school Shirley changed directions, choosing to concentrate in the arts and ending up as the number-one student in her graduating class. The key middle school that she attended was located on the opposite side of Shaoxing from her home, and it took her half an hour by bike to reach there. She was active in sports and in the student union as well. Many years later she married a fellow student from this school.

After completing her school education, Shirley left Shaoxing in fall 1992 to enter the college of foreign languages and literature at Hangzhou University. She majored in English but also studied the Japanese language for two years. Before the amalgamation in 1998 of the six universities to form a multibranched Zhejiang University, Hangzhou University was the sole comprehensive university in the capital city of Zhejiang province and also served as its central teacher-training institution.

Hangzhou University traced its history back to 1897 with the founding of Yuying Academy, which in later years was operated as a private college named Hangzhou Christian University. In 1952, soon after the founding of the People's Republic of China, Zhejiang Teachers College was formed by combining parts of Zhejiang University and Hangzhou Christian University, together with newly established Zhejiang Teachers School and Zhejiang Russian School. Not until May 3, 1958, however, was the name Hangzhou University officially introduced. Shirley received her bachelor's degree in English from Hangzhou University in 1996, and many of her professors now teach in the School of International Studies at Zhejiang University.

She stayed on at the same department for a further three years as a postgraduate student, but she did not sever her ties with her family in Shaoxing. When her father retired in 1997 from his job at the textile factory, she accompanied him on a visit to Beijing, helping him to realize his lifelong travel dream. "Even though my father had only a primary-school education, I have always been close to him and share his values," she made a special point of reporting.

Career

Yet, the life Shirley was beginning to establish in Hangzhou could not have been more different from her parents' lives in Shaoxing. In 1999, she not only received her master's degree in English from Zhejiang University but also got married. Her husband was a young man from Shaoxing who had attended her same senior middle school and had studied international trade as an undergraduate at Zhejiang University. When they married he was working for the government, and through his job they were able to purchase at a subsidized price a newly built apartment in a six-floor walk-up. He, like her, is now a doctoral student at Zhejiang University, having earned a master's degree in economics in 2003. He is employed as a teacher at the Zhejiang University of Finance and Economics.

Shirley was in the process of defining her doctoral research project when I interviewed her. She was interested in the impact of Christian missionary educational methods on present-day Chinese schools. Because Hangzhou had been a center for missionary educational activity before the founding of the People's Republic of China in 1949, her professor in the department of education advised her to investigate this previously unexplored topic. In October 2006, the School of International Studies sponsored an international symposium on Sinology and Sino-West cultural relations and exchanges, for which Shirley presented a paper on her doctoral research.

On July 1, 2003, Shirley gave birth to a baby girl, and her second career, as a mother, began. Normally in China teachers are allowed a three-month maternity leave at a reduced salary. She did not take any leave from her job at Zhejiang University, however. After the summer vacation she returned to teaching classes two mornings a week. In accordance with Chinese traditions, a relative from her husband's side of the family came to live in their apartment to assist with the care of the baby. She mentioned that before the arrival of the baby her husband had been the cook in the family, but now the distant relative does the cooking and cleaning.

After her daughter turned two years old in 2005, Shirley enrolled her in a Zhejiang University-administered day-care facility for which she pays the equivalent of fifty dollars per month. When I asked her whether her daughter enjoyed day care, she admitted that at the very beginning in September the child had cried and cried. "I felt like a cruel mother," she confessed, but her baby soon became accustomed to the routine. Now, when she is delivered at nine o'clock in the morning on Mondays through Fridays, she is happy to take her place among a small group of other two-year-olds. The school day runs until four o'clock in the afternoon. Two teachers care for the class of fewer than twenty children, one tending to their physical needs of washing and feeding, and the other teaching them singing, games and art.

It is a very well-equipped classroom, with a piano and individual tables and chairs and mats for napping. A playground with modern outdoor equipment lies just outside the classroom door. When I accompanied Shirley to her daughter's day care, the young teacher asked me whether I would return the next day to teach the children English. What a prospect: to teach an English lesson to Chinese two-year-olds who are just beginning to speak Mandarin Chinese!

I said, "Yes, I will try." The next morning at 10:00 A.M., I played "Ring Around the Rosy" and sang "Are You Sleeping?" with the thirteen children in the class. By good fortune I learned that a popular Chinese song about two tigers running fast has the same melody as "Are You Sleeping?" I managed to learn this Chinese song before class and sang it together with the Chinese children. Then, the two-year-olds attempted to sing the English words to the same music as in their familiar ditty, "Two Tigers Running Fast." Unfortunately, Shirley had phoned me the night before to inform me of her child's bad cold. Regrettably, her daughter would miss my lesson to her day-care class.

Out of all the young parents whom I met Shirley was one of the few who regretted China's one-child policy. She very much wanted to have a second child, even though she complained about her husband's taking too little responsibility for the care of their daughter. She had been scrutinizing the fine print in the governmental regulations and believed that she had found an exception to which she and her husband's situation belonged. If one of the parents has earned a doctoral degree, then the couple could legally give birth to a second child, she had discovered. This was further motivation for Shirley to complete her Ph.D.

Shao Bin

I met Shao Bin at an art gallery on West Lake, where we both were viewing cartoons by Feng Zikai, a well-known twentieth-century Chinese artist who had lived from 1898 to 1975. One of my colleagues had alerted me to this special exhibit. When I got to the gallery, however, I could not make heads nor tails out of the pictures, because the signs describing both the artist's biography and his works were all written in Chinese characters. A young, thin man approached me and asked whether he could be of assistance. "Yes, thank you," I responded. With his enthusiasm he managed to bring to life each piece of art with its accompanying one-line poem. As we walked around the exhibition rooms, he marveled about how Feng Zikai had been able to transmit artistically an appreciation for the foibles of rural people and animals. "In particular, the artist promoted respect and protection for animals," Shao Bin explained. After an hour or two of intensive art viewing, we both took a city bus back to our

Shao Bin and the author at Zhejiang University of Finance and Economics.

respective apartments and exchanged addresses and phone numbers. Before I left China, Shao Bin presented me with a going-away gift: a book of Feng Zikai's drawings and cartoons.

Childhood

Shao Bin was born in November 1978 in Zhujia, "a small village surrounded by big mountains," as he colorfully described the place. His hometown, which is administered as part of the town of Lijia, is situated in the western reaches of Zhejiang province, not far distant from the Thousand Island Lake and the border with Anhui province. He was the third child of parents who were born in the early 1950s. His two older sisters, both of whom are married and mothers of one son each, still live in the vicinity of the family home; one teaches primary school and the other works in a factory.

His parents own a tiny parcel of rice land (one and a half *mu* or about one-sixth of an acre) and also raise pigs and chickens. His father had worked in Lijia as an accountant for the county government until 1989, so that the family's income was never solely dependent upon agriculture. His grandfather had been employed in the bureau of forestry as a forest guard for more than thirty years. Shao Bin made a point of mentioning that his entire family had helped to support him when he attended middle school.

His early education began at the village primary school in Zhujia, where there were fifty children in each grade. He excelled at school and was one of only two students from all the primary schools within the town of Lijia to gain admission to Yanzhou Middle School, located approximately thirty miles away from his village. This key middle school has a distinguished past, having been established in 1903 in the city of Meicheng, once an important commercial and transport center. To attend this middle school necessitated his becoming a boarder, so that at the age of thirteen he left his family home and went to live in a dormitory room with thirteen other adolescent boys.

The six years he spent as a middle-school student were a formative period, which shaped both his personality and attitudes to life. Yanzhou Middle School opened up to him a world of books and of expanding horizons. Academically, he did very well in Chinese studies and began to learn

117

English but admits that he had found physics difficult. He seemed to be heading toward a future career in the field of humanities. At age fourteen his first piece of writing, a short essay entitled "What is behind the Mountain?" was published in a Chinese-language publication.

His teachers at middle school, especially two in English and a husband and wife pair who taught Chinese, served as a substitute for his own family. The head teacher invited students to his house, where they relaxed and ate ice cream. Shao Bin also enjoyed an active social life at senior middle school, where he participated in the student union and fell in love for the first time. Years later a novel he wrote, called "My Golden Times," depicting a "beautiful, but fragile love story" about his girlfriend at middle school won a writing prize but was never published.

University in Dalian

In 1997, when he was considering where to continue his education, Shao Bin realized that "attending college is a good opportunity to make a dream come true." In his case, he had always longed to have a look beyond the mountains or as he put it, "beyond the horizon, for I like vast and boundless expanses like the sea and sky." For this reason, he chose to study in Dalian, a metropolitan port city in the northeastern region of the country. However, in China a student's score on the college entrance examination actually determines which subject he or she will study, for each university selects its students for various departments according to its own standards. In the case of Shao Bin, he was admitted to Dalian University of Technology but not in the foreign-languages department. Instead, he devoted four "very painful" years to studying chemical engineering with a minor in English. Afterwards, he spent an additional year fulfilling the requirements for a bachelor's degree in English.

Perhaps this unfortunate experience with his course of studies influenced his personal reactions to city life in Dalian. When I met Shao Bin in Hangzhou, he could find few words of praise for this city, which with its scenic beaches, green squares, and vibrant commercial centers is seen by most visitors as an ideal destination. He admitted that he had felt lonely there and, as a southerner, different from the northern Chinese students. He had missed the food and social atmosphere of Zhejiang province. Nevertheless, he remained until spring 2005 at Dalian University of

Technology, completing a master's degree in the Foreign Linguistics and Applied Linguistics program. His research field was translation theory and application.

He was a member of the first class of graduate students at the university's foreign-language school. During those additional two years of graduate studies, Shao Bin developed intellectually in several directions. Poetry, composed in Chinese or in English, was his principal field of study, and he wrote a dissertation about the use of rhyming in translating classical Chinese poetry. He argued in favor of maintaining rhymes, contending that unrhymed English translations are "violations of the original Chinese poems." Yet, he conceded that "imbalanced relationships in meaning, naturalness, style, emotion and rhythm" may occur in a forced use of rhyming and should be avoided as much as possible.

Apart from his research in translation theory, he cultivated other academic interests as well. He discovered the works of a little known American poet from the nineteenth century, Sara Teasdale, whose poetry he wants to introduce to Chinese readers. Her poems about nature especially impress him, and he has translated several of his favorites into Chinese.

When he got a bit bored with translation studies and poetry, he had ventured into a quite unrelated topic of research: lexicology. He enjoyed spending hours surfing the Internet to uncover neologisms or new English words.

Career

After finishing a master's degree in Dalian, Shao Bin at last returned to Zhejiang province to take up employment as a university teacher of English. During early winter 2005, he took the train from Dalian to Hangzhou to interview for jobs at three different universities. He was offered a temporary position at the Zhejiang University of Finance and Economics, an institution newer than Zhejiang University. It opened only thirty years ago at the end of the Cultural Revolution, and its 10,000 students come mainly from Zhejiang province rather than from the whole of China. The original campus, located in northwestern Hangzhou, is in the process of relocating to a recently designated higher-education district in the northeastern part of the city. Already ten other universities, but not

Zhejiang University, have moved to this area, providing facilities for 150,000 students.

When I visited Shao Bin's classroom and office, I was immediately struck by the differences between his facilities and those at the university where I taught. Because the Finance and Economics University had been built in the seventies, there were old-fashioned desks and blackboards, whereas I taught in classrooms with the most up-to-date computer networks and furniture. He explained that at the newly constructed campus of this university, where he has already taught some classes, the equipment is much more modern.

He had signed a one-year contract and his performance was to be assessed at the end of the academic year. He is satisfied with his position, teaching classes in composition and extensive reading to first- and second-year English majors. Class size is comparatively small, with approximately twenty students in each of his four classes, and he finds the students, on the whole, to be enthusiastic and diligent about their studies. For young Chinese interested in careers in finance and economics, a good knowledge of English is a prerequisite. Shao Bin hopes that this temporary job will lead to a three-year contract in the future.

In contrast to Zhejiang University, the foreign languages department at this university offers instruction in only two languages: English and Japanese. As an English teacher at university level, Shao Bin is in a minority in China. Most of his colleagues are female as are the majority of students.

When I met Shao Bin at the art gallery, he had just arrived in Hangzhou from Dalian, and he was still unsure about his housing arrangements. At first, the university had arranged for him to live in an apartment adjacent to the campus where he was teaching. Later, he moved to downtown Hangzhou, where he shares an apartment with a friend from middle-school days. His former classmate works for a state-run company, and housing is included with his job. Shao Bin realizes that this is a temporary arrangement, and bemoans that as a bachelor he is at a disadvantage for university-subsidized housing. There is a waiting list to purchase apartments and priority is given to married couples. He is not especially critical of this policy because he would like to get married, but in the meantime he enjoys his role as uncle to his ten-year-old nephews.

Professionally Shao Bin's first year as a university English teacher in

Hangzhou has been quite successful. Not only has he maintained a busy teaching schedule but he also has completed a full-length (200,000 Chinese characters) manuscript on English neologisms, which Dalian University of Technology Press agreed to publish in 2006. Even though the book is concerned with the English language, I could not read it because he has described in Chinese all his discoveries of new English words. Nevertheless, he outlined the scope of the book for me and provided several examples of the types of neologisms he discusses. "Computer widow," for instance, is an example of a new word from the first part of his book, which he has called combining forms. The second part of the book is devoted to new words on specific topics such as eating or advertisements. "Diet cop" is an example of a neologism that he includes in this section. This work is the product of one and half years of painstaking computer searches, which started out as a diversion and culminated in the publication of his first book, *New English Words Show*.

As is the situation for other young university-level English teachers who were born in the 1970s, Shao Bin realizes that his education will not terminate until he has earned a doctoral degree. Several of his colleagues have enrolled in Ph.D. programs at universities in Shanghai and are pursuing their studies on a part-time basis while working full-time at Zhejiang University of Finance and Economics. He has already started to think about where and with whom he will undertake his doctoral studies. If he pursues further study in the field of translation, he is seriously considering working with his former professor in Dalian, who has now relocated to a university in Suzhou, a city in nearby Jiangsu province.

Alice

Alice was one of the more than twenty graduate students who signed up for my fall seminar on American nonfiction, a course in which the focus was on twentieth-century writers. This seminar was a revised rerun of the class I had given in the spring, but this semester, much to my surprise, some of the students, including Alice, looked older than the master's degree candidates in English literature whom I had taught previously. Appearances were revealing, for I discovered that more than half of those taking the course were full-time English teachers, studying at Zhejiang

University for a master's degree in education. They had taken leaves of absences from their jobs at Chinese schools to attend university classes for one year in Hangzhou. A majority of the English teachers were women and were employed at various schools around Zhejiang province. There were also several male teachers, and a number came from further afield where they taught at either rural or urban schools in the provinces that neighbor Zhejiang, such as Jiangsu and Jiangxi.

These older students changed the dynamics in the seminar. They had never studied postmodern literary theory or feminist thought, but possessed a fount of knowledge about the social and political history of the United States. They were more interested in reading *Roots* by Alex Haley than in discussing Toni Morrison's critical observations about "a black presence" hovering below the surface in the imaginations of American white authors. They could appreciate Rachel Carson's dire warnings about the environmental impact from the overuse of pesticides, but neither the

Alice at Zhejiang University, Zijingang campus.

122

literature students nor the schoolteachers could fathom why Scott and Helen Nearing wanted to *Live the Good Life* in the backwoods of New England. The unanimous refrain I heard from students in the graduate seminars was: "We want to live a well-off life, and the agricultural lives our parents led offer little appeal."

What did appeal to Chinese graduate students was a comparison of the stages of economic prosperity between the United States and China. I would revert to personal stories in these discussions, equating the people in my parents' generation, who had grown up during the 1920s and 1930s, with their own generation, those who had reached maturity in the 1990s or later in China. All of these teachers, who had been born in the '60s or '70s, had grown up in families who had been poor and then had partaken in the spread of prosperity during the 1980s, 1990s, and 2000s. They remembered buying for the first time consumer items such as washing machines, televisions, and cars, and how these purchases impacted the role of women in the household. We discussed *Middletown* by Robert and Helen Lynd that depicted life in Muncie, Indiana, in 1924, and *The Hidden Persuaders,* Vance Packard's critique of psychologically manipulative advertising, published in 1957. They could readily detect elements of Chinese society in these readings about United States society in the twentieth century.

From among the group of teacher graduate students, I became best acquainted with Alice, who teaches English at a senior middle school on an island in southeastern Zhejiang province near to the thriving metropolis of Wenzhou. Outside of the three-hour weekly class sessions, I met her on two other occasions. One time we accidentally passed each other as she was riding her bicycle along one of the tree-lined campus roads and I was walking to my apartment. We exchanged greetings and she told me how much she missed her family back home. She had left behind a husband and six-year-old daughter in order to pursue studies for a master's degree at Zhejiang University.

Then on January 1, 2006, she visited my apartment along with her family. The winter semester had not yet ended, and Alice would not be returning to her hometown until the onset of the Chinese New Year's holiday at the end of January. But her tall, muscular husband, who works as a policeman, had brought their young daughter to Hangzhou to visit her mother, and she wanted to introduce them to me. No one ever entered our apartment without bearing gifts, in true Chinese style. Alice's present was a huge box of pomelos, a famous product from her region of Zhejiang province.

Alice was born in October 1972 in Yuhuan county, one of only twelve island counties and listed among the most economically prosperous counties in China. According to the county's official Website, "In 2002, the comprehensive development of the economy ranked 29th among all the counties in the country." The annual incomes in 2003 of workers in the town ($2211) and farmers in the villages ($903) have made the lives of the 392,800 residents in Yuhuan county more comfortable than for most Chinese. However, the nearly 100,000 migrant workers who have been attracted to this thriving coastal county from provinces in the interior "lead a very poor and unstable life," according to Alice. "Our town-people are relatively richer than they," she said.

Yuhuan owes its comparative wealth to its favorable geographical situation, with a deepwater harbor and first-class fishing port, and also to a well-balanced industrial structure. More than half the population works in the secondary sector, in enterprises that manufacture a range of products from brass valves to air-brake systems to furniture. Another quarter of the population is employed in primary industries such as fish-breeding, forestry, and farming. Orchards of pomelo, a large grapefruit-like fruit, consume one-third of the county's agricultural land. Rice paddies are planted on another half, and the remaining fields produce wheat, cotton, vegetables, and tea. The tertiary sector, including tourism and port activities, absorbs an additional quarter of the workforce. Recuperation and resort centers, where boating, fishing, and beachcombing are popular activities, have brought fame to the county, with Deer Island called "the Jade on the East China Sea." This sobriquet comes directly from the name of the county: the Chinese word *yuhuan* is translated into English as jade bracelet.

As an island county, Yuhuan enjoys ready access to sea transportation, and during the past twenty years an extensive network of roads has connected it to the Taizhou city region to its north. In addition, the airport at Wenzhou is across the bay, which places the county within the reaches of one of the wealthiest regional urban areas in China. Wenzhou, with an urban population of 2,432,000 (2005) within a conurbation that comprises 7.7 million people, has been a principal trading port since the

Tang dynasty. Unfortunately, in August 2006 the thriving city took the brunt of the worst typhoon to hit China in fifty years, suffering casualties of nearly one hundred people, with thousands of houses destroyed.

The historical repute of Wenzhou as a center for commerce and handicrafts and hometown to overseas Chinese has been enhanced in recent decades by its fame as a production base for light industries. Wenzhou is "China's Capital of Shoes," and the full list of goods that are manufactured in this city reads like an industrial catalog, including clothing as its traditional industry, low-voltage electrical equipment, plastic products, printed works, optical glasses, cigarette lighters, valves and pumps, pens, banking equipment, and reciprocating razors. In each of these light industries, the quantities manufactured are massive, and for several of these items Wenzhou's production is the largest in China.

Childhood

Alice, born in October 1972, grew up in a small town in Yuhuan county with two older brothers, one of whom was born in 1958 and the other in 1962. Because of the large age gap between herself and them, she regarded them more as father figures than as siblings. Both brothers went to college and returned to Yuhuan when they began to work. One teaches history at a middle school, and the other is a government official employed by the Bureau of Quality and Technical Supervision.

Her parents were both born in the 1930s, and when she compared their living conditions with her own, she emphasized how "much more hard their lives were than ours now." Her mother was a housewife and skilled tailor, and her father worked as a shop assistant, selling small articles for daily use in another small town.

She described her childhood as "very happy," and recalled spending the whole afternoon digging and playing in the big front garden of her family's two-story house. During the summer holidays she enjoyed "pinching clay figurines, skipping rope, imitating characters in Shaoxing operas, catching mantises." She remembered playing outside until late into the evenings.

Her husband, who grew up in the same area but who was born in 1970, two years earlier than she, recalled "vividly" not having enough to eat as a child. He had accompanied his mother to the seaside to pick discarded corn out of the rubbish and had fought with his three brothers at the dinner table for the largest piece of meat.

Education

Alice attended a nearby primary school that was only a five-to-ten-minute walk from her house. "It was very safe to walk to school with peers," she noted, because "in the early 1980s we seldom saw cars or buses on the roads." At age thirteen she began studying English at Jade City School, the middle school where she now teaches English. In school she "took a liking to music and language," and her ambition was to become a dancer or an interpreter. "However, I didn't have such a chance," she admitted with a touch of sadness.

During her childhood her parents paid tuition to send her to school, the result of the institution of Deng Xiaoping's reform policies. In her estimation, "the money was not much." Today she pays $13 per term for her daughter to attend primary school, but believes that the education her daughter receives is superior to hers. "She can read through easy stories without stopping to ask some unknown words, and she can write some short passages for her summer diary after learning Chinese for only one year." She continued comparing her daughter's schooling with her own, contending that "Now they have more access to information and knowledge than we did. They grasp more skills than we, so they are more clever in their childhood. However, the school burden has become more and more heavy. Sometimes she does not finish her homework until half past eight in the evening. It is hard for a young child to have no time to play." In contrast, Alice mentioned that her mother "was not allowed to go to school when she was young, since women were looked down upon at that time" (i.e., before 1949).

After passing the National College Entrance Examination in 1993, Alice studied for three years at Zhejiang Normal University in the provincial city of Jinhua. This institution, whose status was raised from college to university in 1985, is the key facility for teacher education for Zhejiang province. Initially in 1956, when New China began to fast-track the training of primary and secondary school teachers to staff its burgeoning educational system, the province established Hangzhou Junior Teacher's College. By 1965, with the merger with Zhejiang Physical Education

College, an enlarged Zhejiang Teacher's College was set up and moved to Jinhua. Today Zhejiang Normal University maintains one campus with more than 20,000 undergraduates in the northern suburbs of Jinhua city and another branch campus in Hangzhou.

Jinhua, which is located 115 miles west of Hangzhou in the central part of the province, has had a long and important history as a center of culture and commerce that harkens back 2,000 years. A small-sized Chinese provincial city with a population of 430,000, it serves as a transportation hub for Zhejiang province, connecting highways and railways with coastal and inland areas. The three years that Alice spent as a university student there opened her eyes to a greater Chinese society beyond her island county. In 1996, upon graduation from Zhejiang Normal University as an English major, she was placed in her present job as an English teacher at Jade City Middle School, the same school she had attended as an adolescent.

Career

Not long after Alice assumed her teaching position, she married, at the age of twenty-six, a man from her hometown. Her husband had attended the same middle school as she, and then had furthered his education at the Zhejiang Police Academy. Afterwards, he was assigned to the police force in their hometown and had only recently begun work as a policeman there when they were married.

She gave birth to a daughter on February 15, 1999, and took maternity leave for three months. After the summer holidays, when she went back to teaching, their provision for caring for their child differed from the normal practices in Chinese society. Her husband's relatives did not assume responsibility for their baby. Instead, they employed a babysitter to care for their daughter and to take charge of household chores. They made this decision because her parents-in-law, who lived in another town in Yuhuan county, were still working, and her own parents were already looking after the child of one of her brothers. Years later, in 2005, when Alice took a leave of absence from her job to study at Zhejiang University, her mother-in-law was available to come to their house to take care of her daughter.

Alice is not critical of China's one-child policy. On the contrary, when

I asked about her opinion of the policy, she responded, "It is good because we will have more time and energy to do what we want to and to contribute more to our society. And we will have a better life."

Alice has been teaching English for nine years at Jade City Middle School. In her words, she has experienced

> happiness and sorrow in my teaching. I try to be creative to bridge the state-set teaching goal and the harsh fact that half the students in our school feel at a loss when studying English. Most of the students are studying English to pass examinations; however, I try to keep them interested and make the learning fun.
>
> Our teaching staff has organized various programs to improve the teaching. The teaching materials are always changing, and there have been three changes in the past few years with another new one being introduced in September. The materials are becoming more and more interesting, vivid, communicative and real to life. But to tell the truth, they contain more vocabulary and more passages to read and demand more skills, so that learning becomes more and more difficult for our students. For some students it is really too demanding for them to grasp the usage of words, spelling, grammar and reading skills as well. They gradually lose interest in English, and, to our great sorrow, many of them abandon it.

On at least one memorable occasion, Alice was able to go beyond the state-set curriculum. In December 2001 her school's performance of the musical *The Sound of Music* took first prize in the English entertainment competition sponsored by Taizhou prefecture. She cherishes this event as "a sweet memory for the students and me," because since then no other activities have been undertaken in her prefecture (i.e., school district).

She described this success in an email:

> I couldn't help feeling proud of myself and all the students concerned. Usually teachers don't like this kind of task, for it is so time-consuming and demanding. As you know, all the students are studying for examination papers. The idea of taking part in the rehearsals and performance met a lot of opposition from their parents, although the school was supporting us economically and spiritually.
>
> I was the director and adapted this musical for our students and obtained the music, tape, and video. I chose the right persons for each character among all the students in our school, regardless of their grades, which received support from the school and other teachers. The children danced and sang songs to express their feelings. For

example, a famous song, "Do, Re, Mi," is sung in every household in China. We began to practice the play every day after class. The rehearsals lasted about two or three months. I invited other teachers to watch us and listened to their advice.

Alice had been "longing to undertake further studies at a key university for a long time." When Zhejiang University started the program for the master's degree of education, she applied and received permission from her teaching unit to take the examination. She passed the exam, paid $2500 tuition and enrolled in the program, which required one year of full-time study and residence in Hangzhou and a second year of correspondence courses and the writing of a dissertation. Her thesis will discuss recent research on the teaching of English vocabulary and learning strategies for senior-middle-school students.

During the one-year course of studies at the university, she was required to take classes in a wide range of disciplines that included cognitive linguistics, principles of teaching and learning, cross-cultural communication and translation, modern teaching technologies, testing and teaching, language analysis, scientific communism, and American and British literature. For my class she wrote two term papers: one on Ernest Hemingway's *A Farewell to Arms* and the other on Lorraine Hansberry's *A Raisin in the Sun*.

5

Born in the 1960s and 1950s

Most of the teachers in positions of leadership at Zhejiang University were born during the 1950s and 1960s. I have separated this chapter into two sections, however, to emphasize the distinctions that exist in the career patterns of the '50s and '60s "generations." The younger of the two, those who were born in the 1960s, have been able to follow their own inclinations in making choices in both their personal and working lives. The older generation, those who were born in the 1950s, were able to take advantage of foreign study only after it became widely available during the 1980s. Earlier their education had been disrupted because of the Cultural Revolution. After graduation from university, they were assigned jobs by the government, and for the most part they have remained throughout their careers at their original places of employment.

Each generation has responded differently to the social changes that in many respects have overturned previous ways of eating, dressing, shopping, and getting around the city. Regardless of the decade of their births, one decision in life that everyone shared is adherence to the one-child family. None of the married teachers I met at Zhejiang University had more than one child, with no noticeable preponderance of either boys or girls.

Section 1: Born in the 1960s

We begin with the younger of the two "generations," those who grew up in the midst of the Cultural Revolution but in fact missed most of its impact. They studied at university during the 1980s. As the first generation to respond to the changes that emerged as Chinese society opened up, they have benefited from the opportunities to decide individually about career and personal development. I interviewed two women born in the 1960s, but only Xue-Qun Chen, known to me as Professor Chen, fully disclosed her life's story.

Xue-Qun Chen

We met each other on the school bus to Zijingang campus, the new part of Zhejiang University, where we both taught classes on Tuesday mornings, she in neurobiology and I in Advanced English writing. She hurried onto the bus after I was already seated and asked whether the seat next to me was taken. That was the beginning of a nonstop conversation that ensued during the entire twenty-minute journey to campus, except for her short interruptions to answer her cell phone. In halting English she excitedly described her research about the effects of hypoxia (oxygen deficiency) on the human body, a topic completely unknown to me. After listening to Professor Chen's "research briefing," I too became curious about how people who live in high altitudes with limited supplies of oxygen can adapt to their environments. She pointed out salutary as well as deleterious impacts on the human body from high-altitude living and had expanded my English vocabulary with a new word — hypoxia. For my part, I had committed myself to lecturing to her students about writing scientific papers in English.

Childhood and Education

Xue-Qun Chen was born on June 2, 1963, in the northeastern port city of Dalian in Liaoning province, a region of China that is a part of

Professor Chen at Zhejiang University, Yuquan campus.

what was formerly called Manchuria. She lived there only during the first six years of her life, for her parents resettled in the northwest province of Gansu, where they have remained until today. Both her parents were teachers: her father taught mathematics at Lanzhou Petrochemical College, and her mother taught English in high school. She is their only child.

Xue-Qun's father, who was born in 1926, came originally from southern Hunan province and is a graduate in electrical-machinery engineering from Hunan University in Changsha. Shortly after the founding of New China he moved to Dalian, where he met Xue-Qun's mother, who was a native of that city. She was born in 1935 and studied foreign languages at a teachers' training institution in the same province as her hometown, graduating from Shenyang Normal University, which is located in the capital city of Liaoning province.

Lanzhou, the industrial metropolis and capital city of Gansu province, where Xue-Qun Chen grew up in the 1970s and 1980s, had been designated as one of China's heavy industrial and military centers in the 1950s. Soon after the establishment of the People's Republic of China, priority was placed on the economic development of northwest China, of which Lanzhou in Gansu province forms a critical component. In the late 1960s and early 1970s, when Mao Zedong fashioned what was called a "third-front strategy in China's interior," which involved removing strategic industries away from regions that bordered the Soviet Union and away from coastal or southern areas threatened by the United States, Lanzhou again was favored with large-scale transfers of factories, technicians, and capital.

China built its first large modern oil refinery and petrochemical complex in Lanzhou in the late 1950s. In the 1960s, during the construction there of the giant Liujiaxia dam and hydroelectric power station on the Yellow River, China's mechanical- and electrical-engineering capabilities had advanced to the point that when the dam was completed in 1974, five Chinese-made large hydraulic turbines were capable of generating more than one million kilowatts of electricity. The city assumed central importance in nuclear and missile research and production with the construction of a gas diffusion plant for processing plutonium. Discoveries of significant deposits of nonferrous minerals in Gansu province, especially copper, nickel, and lead, encouraged the establishment of copper smelters, and Liujiaxia-generated electrical power led to Lanzhou's emergence as a prime location for aluminum production.

By the late 1980s, Lanzhou also had developed into a regional trans-portation hub with rail lines that forged links to both eastern and west-ern regions of China. In particular, the railroad connection between Lanzhou and Tianjin, one of China's leading coastal international ports, promoted economic cooperation between these two cities. In addition, the beginnings of a burgeoning air traffic system had been set into motion.

The Yellow River, here narrow and shallow, flows through downtown Lanzhou, and with the city's high elevation at 5,000 feet one might expect a pleasant atmospheric environment. On the contrary, the city lies in a high valley surrounded by barren mountains in close proximity to the Gobi desert, and is reputed to be one of the most polluted places in China. But in the eyes of American sinologist A. Doak Barnett, who wrote of his visit to Lanzhou in 1988, "The general ambience was not totally unattrac-tive. Few factory districts in any country are really attractive, but I was impressed that this area was less grimy than many I have seen elsewhere.... The streets were generally quite wide, and most were lined with trees.... Massive blocks of workers' apartments, all of them several stories high, were well built and clean" (*China's Far West: Four Decades of Change*, Boulder, CO: Westview Press, 1993, p. 194).

Xue-Qun's parents arrived in Lanzhou as part of a government-planned migration of people from more economically advanced areas in the east to northwest China. Her father came to teach at Lanzhou's Petro-chemical College, which was founded in 1956 to train local engineers, technicians, and scientists to manage the rapidly increasing number of heavy industrial enterprises.

By the time his daughter was old enough to attend university in the early 1980s, an educational institution less tied to industrialization offered a new option for further study. "My parents advised me to study at the College of Traditional Chinese Medicine, which had opened up only in 1977," Professor Chen told me. "They said that it sounded interesting." Women comprised half the student body, and the curriculum offered courses in both Western and Chinese medicine.

When she began her studies there, Xue-Qun had intended to become a teacher. Up to that period in her life she had not been especially aca-demic, and when I asked her about her interests in college, she mentioned only sports. Yet, she changed fundamentally during those four years. As she put it, "I wanted to know why things happened." In other words, she started to think like a scientist and she has never changed course. As an undergraduate she took classes in physiology as well as in traditional medicine, and she spent one year in practice at a hospital of Chinese medicine. Afterwards, she continued her training for an additional half-year at the Traditional Chinese Medicine College in Nanjing, the leading institution in this field.

She earned a bachelor of science degree in 1985 and remained at the college in Lanzhou for an additional three years, employed as an assistant professor in the department of basic medical sciences. During this time she met a young chemistry graduate student, who had also grown up in western China and who was studying at Lanzhou University, one of the first universities in China to enroll bachelor's, master's and doctoral degree candidates. This venerable higher-educational institution, founded in 1909, had distinguished itself in the natural sciences by placing emphasis on basic theoretical research. When this young man, named Wang Yang Guang, completed his Ph.D. degree in chemistry in 1988, the two were married. At the age of twenty-five Xue-Qun left behind her parents and her childhood in Lanzhou.

The couple moved to Tianjin, the eastern coastal city that had developed close economic ties with Lanzhou, where her husband was employed in the chemistry department at Tianjin University. Here, she embarked on the next stage of her education, pursuit of a master of science degree in the department of basic medical sciences at the Traditional Chinese Medicine University in Tianjin. Her studies involved experimental research with acupuncture, and she completed a dissertation on the effects of electro-acupuncture on the healing of gastric ulcers in rats in 1991.

They remained in Tianjin for two more years, during which time she worked as a lecturer and assistant professor in the same department in which she had received her master's degree. In addition, on December 8, 1991, Xue-Qun Chen gave birth to a baby girl. When I became acquainted with Xue-Qun in 2005, this baby was now a teenager and arguing with her teacher about hair styles. According to her mother, as a typical early adolescent the girl was "really stubborn." Professor Chen never introduced her to me.

Soon after the baby's birth, her father and aunt moved to Tianjin to offer assistance in caring for the baby. Her father, rather than her mother, came to help out because he had already retired, whereas her mother was still employed as a schoolteacher in Lanzhou.

Career

After spending five years in Tianjin, Xue-Qun Chen's husband transferred his job to Zhejiang University, where he joined the chemistry department. This move came about because of the beneficence of his supervising professor, whom Zhejiang University had personally recruited to join the faculty, and who had invited Dr. Wang Yang Guang, her husband, to follow him to Hangzhou. This change dramatically altered the career paths of both husband and wife. In 2005, when they were still in their forties, Dr. Wang had risen to chairman of the chemistry department, and Professor Chen had become an associate professor in neurobiology in the College of Life Sciences at Zhejiang University.

During their twelve years in Hangzhou, however, there had been ups and downs in Xue-Qun Chen's career, and her initial response to the city had not been especially positive. On arriving in 1993, she was unemployed and overwhelmed by the responsibility of caring for a young child. The family moved into an apartment in the "faculty village," a housing compound that consists of many blocks of four-and five-story buildings located directly across the road from the university's Yuquan campus. She enrolled her daughter in the university's day-care facility and found an administrative job at the university's school of medicine. She felt dissatisfied and complained about the "dirtiness" of Hangzhou. Eventually, she returned to the same type of teaching and clinical work that had engaged her in Tianjin and became employed as an assistant professor in the medical university's department of basic medical sciences.

It was not until 1996 that she was able to identify her real calling. The research work she had carried out for her master's degree had been in the field of acupuncture, for which she had studied physiology and the functioning of the nervous system. In 1996 she had heard that a famous neurobiologist named Dr. Ji-Zeng Du, a member of the Chinese Academy of Sciences from Xining in Qinghai province, had been invited to establish a new laboratory in the College of Life Sciences at Zhejiang University. From the day she learned about Professor Du's imminent arrival in Hangzhou until mid–1997, when she had her first interview with him,

Xue-Qun Chen pursued a course of intensive reading in his field of science, namely neurobiology. She also contacted her former supervisor at the Traditional Chinese Medicine University in Tianjin, who had graduated with Professor Du from Beijing University in the late 1950s. She asked him for an academic recommendation, making use of "*guanxi*," the Chinese word for "pull" in English.

In August 1997 her enterprising efforts proved to be successful, and Xue-Qun Chen began her doctoral program under the direction of Professor Du. This course of study ideally combined her personal inclinations for the subject matter with her preparatory educational background. Her connection with Professor Du also brought together two generations of Chinese scientists.

Professor Du had been recognized as a brilliant young man when New China was beginning to create a system of institutions for scientific research. In the early 1960s the Chinese government sent him from Beijing to northwest China, specifically to Xining in Qinghai province, which is located to the west of Lanzhou. In this area of high elevation he set up a neurobiological laboratory. After thirty-three years in this remote region of China, interrupted by only one three-year research assignment in California during the 1980s, he began afresh in the mid–1990s at Zhejiang University. Professor Chen, who is twenty-five years his junior, had spent nearly twenty years as a child and young woman in this same high-altitude, western area of the country. How fitting that they should collaborate in research on the effects of hypoxia, a condition that affects people who reside in high-altitude locales.

Xue-Qun Chen completed her Ph.D. in 2000, writing a dissertation on the regulation of hypothalamus neuropeptides in rats during hypoxia stress. Since 2001, she has managed the laboratory for the division of neurobiology at Zhejiang University and has taught undergraduate as well as graduate courses in brain science, molecular neurobiology, and neurobiology. As a research scientist, she has published numerous articles in international journals on her experiments on the effects of hypoxia in rats and mice and recently has begun to present papers at international conferences.

Professor Chen has continued to focus her research on the branch of neurobiology that deals with the adaptation of animals to a limited supply of oxygen. Her experiments have been funded by research grants awarded by the Natural Science Foundation of China that support the laboratory at Zhejiang University. In 2005, for the first time, she received her own grant from the Chinese Natural Science Foundation to study hormonal treatments for the condition of hypoxia anorexia in rats.

Whenever I met Professor Chen on the street, often when she was riding her bicycle back or forth from the lab, she would enthuse about her research findings. Did I realize that new-born babies could have their learning and memory functions enhanced by exposure to hypoxia? Did I know that hypoxia, when combined with cold temperatures and psychological stress, could create extremely negative reactions?

Her research topic that most intrigued me concerned the Tibetan antelope. What enables this animal to run so fast when it dwells in a high-elevation environment with limited supplies of oxygen? She posed this question at a particularly opportune time, for this animal was one of those under consideration as a mascot for the Beijing Olympics in 2008. As it turned out, the Tibetan antelope was one of five so-called *Fuwa* that the Chinese Olympic Committee diplomatically adopted as a group of Olympic mascots. Now her scientific findings in basic research may turn out to be newsworthy to the general public.

When I visited her laboratory and the class that she asked me to teach, I was able to observe that her field of science, neurobiology, was not gender-skewed in China. I learned that biology was a popular major for women undergraduates and discovered that seven out of the eighteen graduate students in neurobiology were women. She was advising her students to follow in her footsteps and to remain in basic research. "When you go to work for a pharmaceutical company, you may earn more money, but it is difficult to publish original research, because your results belong to the company," she argued. And for Professor Chen, research is at the center of her life. Her husband drives a car, but she prefers to ride a bicycle to her laboratory. On the day of my departure from China she told me that she was about to leave for Hong Kong to spend a six-day holiday with her family. "My daughter will enjoy it," she remarked, as she hurried back to her lab.

Yang li-qiu

Another person born in the 1960s whom I interviewed is the external relations officer at the School of International Studies at Zhejiang

University. I first met Madame Yang (that is how I addressed her) on the Internet six months before I arrived in Hangzhou. She was the person who made all my living arrangements for the year I spent in China. It was she who had replied to my anxious email messages about administrative delays, visa matters, travel, post, and other concerns, always counseling me to remain patient.

I did not realize until I met her informally during a university-arranged weekend excursion to a scenic region in Zhejiang province that she had been a professor of English before assuming her administrative position. "Now I understand why your English is so good," I exclaimed to Madame Yang as we sat on a log watching acrobats maneuver along a tight rope strung high up between two mountain cliffs.

She proceeded to relate her abbreviated biography, which entirely altered the image I had created of Madame Yang during those nerve-wracking months of waiting to leave for China. She had graduated as an English major from Jilin Normal University in 1986. The northeastern province of Jilin, where she was born, is part of the former region of Manchuria.

When she completed her studies she had married another English major. Her husband, who had grown up in Zhejiang province, graduated from the Foreign Language University in Beijing. Together they volunteered to accept assignments at a university in Llasa, the capital city of Tibet. They lived there on the campus for eight years, during which time she taught English and he was employed in administration. "We really liked Tibet and are planning to visit again this summer, traveling on the newly opened train line," she added in an excited voice. "Everyone was very friendly and the city, situated in a valley surrounded by hills, is very beautiful. We had a dog, which my husband especially enjoyed, and we saw yaks, Tibetan antelope, deer." She admitted that it had taken them a while to accustom themselves to eating Tibetan food, but eventually they learned to relish the fried pancake that is a mainstay of the diet there. When I asked her about her colleagues at the university, she replied that most teachers in the English department were non–Tibetan. She recalled a few local residents who were teachers, as well as several Westerners. After we returned from the weekend excursion, she brought to her office a group photograph that had been taken of the English department, which illustrated the diversity of the teaching faculty.

In 1988 she returned temporarily to Jilin to give birth to a son, whom she left behind in the care of her family during his infancy. Eventually, when he turned three years old, she brought him to Tibet. In 2005 this son was completing his last year of high school in Hangzhou.

When they left Tibet in 1994, the family moved to Hangzhou, the capital city of her husband's home province. She changed her occupation at that time, transferring from university teaching to administration, and her husband left the university altogether to take up employment in finance. Having been born in the 1960s, they reached maturity after the Chinese economy had opened up, and she and her husband were able to take advantage of new employment options as they became available. They also could continue to satisfy their wanderlust, for they both still enjoy traveling. She listed several other major trips around China that they have undertaken after their departure from Tibet.

Section 2: Born in the 1950s

University teachers whom I interviewed who were born in the 1950s had experienced personal histories more tumultuous than those of the younger generation of teachers previously described. They had grown up during the 1960s and 1970s, when politics had impacted strongly upon individual lives and when the standard of living had been considerably lower. For the most part, they had not been responsible for making decisions about their careers but had been assigned to their teaching posts. I had conversations at Zhejiang University with several English professors from this generation, but only one man, whom I called Ian, revealed his full biography. Ian also introduced me to his wife and eleven-year-old daughter. This section will focus on his personal history.

Ian

I met Ian, a tall attractive man in his early fifties, for the first time on the school bus. Not until several months later, while touring a nearby

historical town together with Ian and his daughter was I able to appreciate his stories about his early years growing up in Ningbo, the second
largest city in Zhejiang province. Many of the sights we visited during
that day-long excursion to Wuzhen, a popular Zhejiang tourist destination, reminded him of his own house, clothes, food and of the events of
his youth.

Childhood and Education

As one of six children, Ian, who was born in July 1953, spent his
childhood residing in a house in Ningbo's city center. His father's occupation was shop assistant and his mother worked in a factory, but before
the founding of the People's Republic of China his family had managed a
small business. His grandfather had owned a retail food store, and after
his death two of his sons had formed a partnership that later was dissolved.
As an indication of his ancestral family's bourgeois origins, Ian mentioned
that his grandmother had bound feet. He elaborated upon this aspect of
his past, relating that "During the Cultural Revolution we searched for
any of her old shoes that still remained in the house and made sure that
we burned them." When I visited his Hangzhou apartment, he drew attention as well to a few pieces of antique furniture that he had salvaged from
his childhood home.

Ningbo enjoys a long history as a city. Because it is situated on a large
river only twelve miles from the coast, its past is coupled to its role as an
important domestic and international port. It occupies a central position
along the coastline of China, directly south of the Yangtze River delta.
Archeologists have found remains there of a settlement belonging to the
Neolithic Hemudu Culture from seven thousand years ago, and historical
records show that by 200 B.C. sailors were already embarking from Ningbo
for journeys to other countries. In the Tang dynasty in the seventh century a lively coastal trade in agricultural produce and dried seafood had
developed. There were portents, as well, of its future international
significance when emissaries from Japan and Korea on diplomatic mis-
sions to the Tang court chose Ningbo as their port of entry.

Portuguese merchants in the sixteenth century were the first Westerners to start trading at Ningbo, followed soon after by the Dutch and
later the British, making use of one of the largest customhouses in China.

After the defeat of China in the Opium War in 1842, Ningbo was designated as one of five international treaty ports, and became home to an "extraterritorial" British community of merchants and missionaries under the protection of a Western legal system. In 1860 during the Taiping Rebellion, France stationed military troops there to protect its trading privileges. In the nineteenth and early twentieth centuries Ningbo businessmen gained wide repute for their talents in providing financial services, but the port's shipping and storage capabilities failed to compete with those at nearby Shanghai.

During Ian's childhood years in Ningbo, from 1953 to 1978, the fortunes of the city and its port facilities had diminished considerably. Ningbo had fallen back into the shadows of both the provincial capital Hangzhou, about ninety miles to the west, and of the nearby metropolis of Shanghai across Hangzhou Bay to the north. At the time Ian left the city, the urban population barely reached half a million and the economy was dominated by comparatively small-scale consumer industries, particularly textiles and food processing. Not until the 1980s did the city of Ningbo begin to gain national stature as a desirable exporting location, and today its deepwater, ice-free harbor ranks second in China after Shanghai in tonnage of cargo handled. When the twenty-two mile long bridge over Hangzhou Bay opens in 2008, driving time between Ningbo and Shanghai will be reduced to one and a half hours. Zhejiang province's second city, with a population of more than two million, is looking forward to asserting its strength as an economic powerhouse once again.

In the 1960s, Ian attended primary school in Ningbo and did well in school. He was head student and served as class monitor. He was the most academically minded of the six children in his family, and the only one to make a career in education. Because his sisters were encouraged out of financial necessity to start work at a young age, none of them remained at school, even though his oldest sister had always enjoyed reading. His one brother, who now works at a hotel in Hangzhou, did not receive a higher education. One of Ian's sisters never married and came to Hangzhou to live with his family when his daughter was an infant. The others have raised their own families and have continued to reside in other nearby cities in Zhejiang province. After his parents died (mother in the 1980s and father in the 1990s), Ian's ties to Ningbo were severed. Only in 2007, with his appointment as dean of the School of Foreign Languages

Studies at Ningbo Institute of Technology, was he reconnected again with his hometown.

His family lived in a wooden house in the center of Ningbo, which was sizeable enough to share with another family. When I toured Wuzhen, the Zhejiang provincial town where the writer Mao Dun had grown up, Ian commented that the houses we saw there reminded him of his childhood home. "I like them very much," he repeated often throughout that day. To enter a house you had to step over a ledge, and the various rooms were separated from one another by open-air patios. His family's house lacked toilet facilities and everyone used a bucket. They did not own a well but relied on collecting rainwater in basins. Although there was electricity, they cooked meals on a wood-burning stove and did not buy a television set until the late 1970s. Ian remembers living "very frugally" as a child, stressing in particular that the family's diet did not include eating meat every day: "We bought food with coupons and subsisted on various types of vegetables, eggs, and rice." In Wuzhen, as well as at other traditional venues in and around Hangzhou, street vendors sold a snack food called "stinky tofu," which is fermented tofu cooked over an open fire. Ian had relished this "treat" as a child.

After he finished primary school, with the onset of the Cultural Revolution in 1966, the academic content of Ian's school education was deemphasized, according to his recollection. He learned carpentry, went to the countryside to help with the harvest, and was a "little Red Guard." At home, on the other hand, he always liked to read books and remembers doing his own science experiments.

When I asked him how and when he started to study English, he told me that while he was in middle school, a friend of his, the son of a teacher who knew English, had lent him books. After President Nixon's trip to China in 1972, more opportunities to study the English language became available. He reminisced nostalgically about reading and rereading to the point of memorizing every page from a textbook called *English 900,* leaving the book in tatters from wear. In 1973 he was chosen to participate in an one-year English-language course.

Not until he was twenty-five years old, however, was he able to take the college-entrance examination enabling him to acquire a higher education. Until then he had remained at home in Ningbo, where he worked for one year as an electrician in a factory and then taught junior middle school. In September 1978 he boarded a boat for Shanghai, where he enrolled as an undergraduate in the department of English language and literature at Shanghai International Studies University. This university had been established by the Ministry of Education in 1949 as the Shanghai College of Russian. Today it offers instruction in fourteen languages: English, German, French, Russian, Japanese, Arabic, Spanish, Italian, Greek, Portuguese, Korean, Persian, and Thai in addition to Chinese.

Career

After four years of study and the completion of a bachelor's degree, he received his work assignment. At age 29, in 1982, Ian launched a career as a teacher of general English and linguistics at Zhejiang University in Hangzhou. He joined what was called an English language teaching group that predated the setting up of a separate department of English in 1984. In the 1950s, Zhejiang University had been designated as an institution with a focus on science and technology instruction and research, and when Ian arrived, Russian was the principal foreign-language course offering. He shared housing with another new-hire, a young man who also had just graduated as an English major and who, along with Ian, was still employed as an English teacher at Zhejiang University in the year 2005.

During his first few years on the job Ian, together with other English teachers, devised an English-language curriculum appropriate for Zhejiang University, and he taught a wide range of language and linguistics courses. He recalled that the classrooms were shabbily equipped and even dirty. Some of his teaching took place at another campus, the former private Christian college called Zhijiang University, where first and second year students were housed.

Then in 1985 Ian's career prospects suddenly changed. He won a one-year scholarship to study for a master's degree in England. In relating to me the excitement that he had felt when he heard the news twenty years ago, it was as if he were reliving those moments: "I never imagined that I would go there." His previous experience of the language had been only indirect. He had studied English from textbooks, had read the classics of English literature, had learned about Karl Marx's London, and had listened to English-language radio broadcasts.

From 1985 to 1986 he studied linguistics at the University of Leeds and wrote a master's dissertation entitled "English Passives and Chinese Counterparts." Perhaps even more life-changing for him was the opportunity to travel both in the British Isles and on the European continent and to meet English people. A family invited him to visit their house in Manchester on many occasions, and he toured around Britain, making sure that he found Marx's desk at the British Museum. I asked him whether life in England in the mid–1980s had surprised him, recalling anecdotes that I had heard about young Chinese students in England shocked at their first sight of a vacuum cleaner. But he replied in the negative: "I wasn't surprised, because I had read about English life for years before I had the chance to observe it firsthand."

On returning to China, he started writing journal articles and translating from Chinese into English for Zhejiang University, while continuing to teach a full schedule of classes in English-language instruction. His first publications dealt with topics on the teaching of foreign languages: one published in 1987 on the use of authentic materials, and another published in 1988 on computer-assisted language learning.

Ian's professional career expanded in another direction when he began to assume administrative responsibilities. In 1989 he was asked by the Ministry of Education to serve as chief examiner on the National Education Examinations Authority. At the same time he increased his managerial role in the department of English at Zhejiang University. By 1995 he had been appointed vice dean of the Department of Foreign Language Studies, a position he held both before and after the merger of Hangzhou's universities in 1998. After seven years at this job, he realized that his genuine interests were in research and writing and he resigned as vice dean.

Ian's academic focus shifted somewhat during the 1990s after he completed a second master's degree in England. For one year, from October 1991 to October 1992, he studied Teaching English for Specific Purposes at the University of Exeter, and received a master of education degree for a dissertation entitled "A comparative investigation into journal article abstracts written by native speakers in English and Chinese." After his return to China he became a tutor in the master's program in linguistics and applied linguistics at Zhejiang University, and turned his attention increasingly toward research into foreign-language teaching methods. He wrote articles on topics such as "Action research in foreign language education" and "An empirical study of group work in the English class-room," and started to publish textbooks for teaching English to Chinese students. He coauthored two books: in 1994, a coursebook and in 1997, *Survival English 100*. Then, in 1998, Zhejiang University Press published *Using English Grammar*, the first book for which he was sole author.

He also started to collaborate with colleagues in England and Hong Kong, beginning as a team member in a three-year research project (1996–99) on the China Public English Test System, which was jointly funded by the Chinese Ministry of Education and the Department for International Development in Britain. Research work for this project led him back to England, where he spent November and December 1997 at the University of Cambridge. He has continued to participate in cooperative studies with professors at the Chinese University of Hong Kong on "English reading research." In his recent textbook *Practical English Writing* he acknowledges close collaboration with a colleague from the City University of Hong Kong. Concurrently he has been involved in numerous research projects on English testing and teaching sponsored by Zhejiang provincial authorities and by the Chinese Ministry of Education.

In February 2005, Higher Education Press in Beijing published Ian's book entitled *Practical English Writing*, intended as an aid for Chinese who need to compose job applications and academic research papers. This comprehensive writing guide, marketed as both a coursebook and a handbook, includes a CD-ROM containing PowerPoint lecture slides as well as a learning pack of exercises in grammar and the mechanics of writing. As he describes in the foreword, this book grew out of "a very well-received English writing course" that he had initiated in 2001 for graduate and undergraduate students at Zhejiang University, motivated by students' changing purposes for writing in English: "In recent years, with the implementation of the country's policy of reform and opening to the outside world, many people can now realize their dreams to further their studies abroad and to work in multi-national corporations or joint ventures. Hence, these materials take the form of writings for the purpose of academic and job applications." In 2007, Ian came out with a second reference book for Chinese readers about writing in English. This new book, entitled *Research Paper Writing*, was published by Zhejiang University Press.

Family Life

Ian waited to marry until he returned from his second year of study in England at the end of 1992. He married a woman who was born in 1957 and was working as a physician in Hangzhou. She had come to Zhejiang University to study medicine, and afterwards was placed as a doctor at a medical facility for army veterans that is located near West Lake. As she does not speak English, I relied on him to provide her biographical details. He mentioned more than once that his wife had grown up in an intellectual family, with a father who was a medical doctor and a mother who was a nurse. "She really did not have a hometown," he explained, "because the family moved to where they were assigned by the government." She had attended school in Hefei, the capital of Anhui province, but because her mother had come originally from Nanjing she had learned to cook in a Nanjing style.

In 1994, she gave birth to their only child. When I became acquainted with Ian's family in 2005, their tall and unusually attractive daughter was attending grade six, her final year of primary school. She is especially interested in art, and when I visited the family's apartment, she had many of her own illustrations of fashionably dressed women decorating her room. After she was born, Ian's unmarried older sister came to live with them and stayed for three years, providing assistance in a household in which both parents were working full time.

In the 1990s the three adults and child in Ian's household shared a small apartment in the same faculty village in which Professor Chen, her husband and her daughter resided. Most faculty members of Zhejiang University whom I met lived in this same community, which consisted of apartment blocks built along narrow, tree-lined lanes. Surrounding the village on two sides are rows of small shops, and on another side a day-care center and primary school are conveniently situated. The other campuses of Zhejiang University housed faculty in similar complexes, but at least one English professor whom I visited had bought a luxurious and large new apartment located in a fast-developing district in northwest Hangzhou.

In 2003, after waiting for almost ten years, Ian was able to purchase a newly constructed two-bedroom apartment in the same faculty-housing village for $17,500. It is on the fifth floor of a no-elevator building and is fully equipped with modern appliances. Lacking only are a dishwasher and clothes dryer, two Western products that have not yet been incorporated into Chinese lives. He pointed out that if the university had not subsidized the sale, the market price for this apartment would have been $37,500. Not included is parking space for a car. For Ian that poses no problem, for he continues to be satisfied to ride a bicycle in the neighborhood and to use taxis and buses for travel further afield. Not all faculty members share his opinion, however, and cars are beginning to clutter many pedestrian lanes in the village.

Often when I got together with Ian he brought along his daughter, who was already studying English in primary school. She would sit on the back of his bicycle or she would quietly eat tangerines or drink yoghurt when we were together, but she was reluctant to speak in English. Because he was a professor of English, I think that he supposed that his daughter would gravitate naturally to the English language, and he took every opportunity to encourage her to practice it. Eventually, I visited her English class and met her best friend as well, as described in chapter 6, "Born in the 1990s."

Ian's daughter's childhood could not have been more different from his own, even though both were spent in urban Zhejiang province. He was born in the 1950s, when his family, in his own words, "lived frugally." His strong determination to study English in the midst of the Cultural Revolution propelled him to embark on an academic career as a university professor. When we toured a Taoist temple in Wuzhen, Ian was reluctant for his daughter to stand in line to have her fortune told. Having grown up in Mao's China, he as father to a preadolescent child born in the 1990s sometimes found it difficult to accept every aspect of culture available in present-day Chinese society. Will Ian's daughter become a fashion designer? Only time will tell.

Other English Professors

I interviewed two other professors of English at Zhejiang University who were born in the 1950s, one whom I called Johnson and the other Ann. Because they had lived through the same revolutionary changes in Chinese society that Ian had experienced, they shared similar biographies, but in some other respects they each expressed varying opinions. In contrast to Ian, both had grown up in Hangzhou and had studied at university there. Each had married at an earlier age than Ian and were parents of one child who had been born in the 1980s.

Ann

Ann started teaching English at Zhejiang University in 1982, the same year that Ian began and she also attained an upper management position in the foreign-language department. Like Ian, she had waited for several years after finishing her school education in 1974 to enter university, because of the absence of college-entrance examinations. When I asked her how she had spent those years, her only reply was that she had stayed at home and had worked at part-time jobs. She entered Zhejiang University as an undergraduate in 1978 and was assigned to work as a teacher there after completing her studies.

Today she has been able to take advantage of new employment opportunities for women in Chinese universities. Her husband, who works for an oil company, also has adapted himself to the opened-up economy. Her eighteen-year-old son boards at senior high school number 2 in Hangzhou. I never met either her husband or her son, but she was filled with praise for her son's academic achievements and was encouraging his ambitions toward a scientific career. I asked her whether she missed having her son at home during his formative years as an adolescent, and she replied that boarding school had made him independent and able to mature at a younger age.

Johnson

Johnson's account of his life during the Cultural Revolution sounded very different from the way Ian described his. During the late 1960s Johnson had spent three years working in the countryside outside of Hangzhou. "I did all sorts of work and found it to be a rich personal experience," he told me. He believes that young people growing up in today's China are spoiled and would be better off if they too could see for themselves and appreciate how rural people live. The spiraling income gap between rich and poor concerns him very much. He is convinced, however, that "the problem lies with local authorities who do not implement the excellent policies that the central government has devised. That's not the way it was when Mao Zedong was leader; Mao was a very powerful man," Johnson argues.

He started studying English at Hangzhou University in 1973, at a time when I presumed that Chinese universities were still in the throes of educational disruption. When I asked him about my quandary, he explained that by that date the Cultural Revolution in Hangzhou was mostly over. Nonetheless, students were admitted to universities without taking the college-entrance examination. After finishing his undergraduate degree he began his career as an English-language teacher at Hangzhou University, an institution which in those years primarily trained teachers. In the 1980s he continued his study of English in Australia for two years, participating in the first wave of Chinese studying abroad.

Johnson married a woman who worked as an assistant at a hospital, and in 1984 their only child was born, a son who is now studying economics at a university in Ningbo. Ten years ago he bought an apartment "very cheaply" in the faculty village, and like Ian, he has no interest in purchasing a car. He continues to get around on a bicycle. But unlike Ian, who has created a CD-ROM appendix for his newly-published English-language textbook, Johnson does not use a computer.

In fact, he prefers many aspects of the past. At the end of the academic year, when fourth-year students were anxiously arranging job interviews, Johnson compared the present situation with the way it used to be. "The planned economy was much better for getting jobs. Until the late 1990s graduates did not find their own employment. After they completed their studies their class leader handed out assigned positions in a factory, government office or at a school or college."

PART THREE:
FACES OF THE FUTURE

Children born in the 1990s and in the first decade of the twenty-first century are confronting an environment in China much changed from earlier decades. Their society is more affluent and more confident of its national identity and position in the world. It also is more divided between haves and have-nots.

Increased prosperity is apparent in the greater availability and variety of material goods but also in the changing lifestyles of Chinese people. For the most part, they enjoy adequate supplies of food and decent places to live. Television, telephones, T-shirts, jeans, and the English language have been a part of their lives from infancy. One of my university students told me that when her aunt was pregnant she kept listening to English songs, which she called antenatal instruction. The five-year-old child now knows hundreds of English words and can say easy sentences, which pleases her parents. Families eat out at restaurants and take holidays by train and bus to visit tourist and natural sites. For the very affluent, there has been a growth in international travel destinations. Although everyone works very hard, leisure activities have begun to make headway into people's lives.

For children growing up these changes present new opportunities for future careers. Whereas today engineers are needed in every productive sector of the industrial economy, in ten or twenty years' time service-sector employment may be more in demand. Children today dream about becoming a backpacker or fashion designer.

No longer is China a closed society, fearful of cultural influences from abroad. Through the media and the Internet, children are exposed to global trends in music, film, literature, art and fashion from an early age. Instead of Western culture being absorbed as a one-way sieve, however, appreciation for Chinese traditions is much in evidence around the world. Architects and landscape designers are aware of Chinese aesthetic concepts, and even hairdressers in the United States use *feng shui* beauty products. Chinese calligraphy classes have become popular in many countries, and Chinese medical practices as well as medicines have been widely accepted as alternative methods for curing diseases.

Yet, underlying the visible transformations in Chinese society lies a yawning disparity in wealth that keeps widening despite continuous efforts by the government to reverse the situation. Families of children in urban areas enjoy incomes 3.2 times higher than families in rural areas. A geographical divide exists as well. Eastern China is much more prosperous than western China, a phenomenon left over from the early years of

Sixth-grade class at Affiliated Primary School of Zhejiang University, Hangzhou.

market-opening to the world when cities along the east coast led the movement toward economic reform.

Salaries in most fields have climbed, but the gap between the top earners and those at the bottom inches up from year to year. Wages for migrant workers, people pushed out of the countryside and pulled toward urban areas, also show income disparities. Jobs in eastern China pay 14 percent more than in the western regions of China (*China Daily* online, February 2, 2007).

Though babies wherever they live in China still toddle around in open-bottomed clothes without diapers, the differences between the lives of city and rural children are wide and ever expanding. While urban parents pay hundreds of dollars to send their obese children to slimming summer camps, a migrant worker and father of a 21-month-old son was quoted in *China Daily* (January 23, 2006) as he was about to board a train in Beijing bound for his mountain village in Guizhou province: "To be honest with you, I'm very envious of the city dwellers' life. They have a decent job and can entertain themselves as they wish after work. I hope my son can lead such a life."

This final part of the book focuses on China of the future. Chapter 6, "Born in the 1990s," presents a close-up view of the ways that children are growing up in the family and at school. I interviewed two girls, ages seven and eleven, and also visited Chinese schools where I taught English classes to children from age two to seventeen.

The concluding chapter details how China is building for the future and confronting societal problems of today. Seven topics, namely health care, social security, education, environmental protection, family planning, governmental management and rural development are discussed as well as some of the attempted solutions. In both chapters in this part of the book, essays written by university students illustrate the vision of those who will be the central actors in China of the twenty-first century.

6

Born in the 1990s

Children growing up in China today are experiencing childhoods vastly different from those of their parents. What were once considered "decadent ideas and lifestyles" have become normal ways of living for children born in the 1990s. They eat fast food, listen to rock music, read *Harry Potter* translated into Chinese, take photos with digital cameras, play computer games and basketball, and chat online. Plastered on walls of buildings are advertisements for beauty products and photos of basketball star Yao Ming, instead of big red banners proclaiming a thought of Mao Zedong.

The media continually run reports about "pampered Chinese children" being raised in one-child families in which not only parents but also both sets of grandparents cater to the children's needs. They are commonly referred to as "little emperors." At the same time, Chinese journalists write about children's increased sense of angst due in part to anxieties about their parents' future welfare, the responsibility for which rests on their shoulders alone.

My information on the youngest sector of Chinese society, those born in the 1990s, comes from a variety of sources. I was able to piece together biographies of two of the children of adults whom I interviewed: the daughter of Ian, the English professor (see chapter 5); and the daughter of the pharmacist couple in Anhui province and cousin to Fan Gao, the rural university student (see chapter 2). Even though children as young as

155

two years old would call out "hello" from across the street, and one of the neighbor boys introduced himself to me as he walked to school, conducting in-depth interviews with others of his generation was constricted by my limited knowledge of the language.

My other entrée into learning about the lives of Chinese children came from my contact with Chinese schools. I taught English-language classes at three different schools in Zhejiang province: the Affiliated Primary School of Zhejiang University, Daguan Middle School in northwest Hangzhou, and Deqing Vocational School. On these occasions I met children in grades six, seven, and ten and was introduced to the public school system. In addition, penetrating personal essays written by my university students on the assigned topic, "Chinese education," opened another window onto Chinese school life.

Cindy

I first met Ian's daughter, whose English name is Cindy, when he brought her along on one of his frequent visits to our apartment. She is an unusually tall and attractive girl of eleven, who was completing her last year of primary school in 2005. She would sit quietly at the table while her father and I conversed in English. Although she had been studying English in school for three years she was hesitant to speak to me and I was not sure how much she understood of our conversations. By nature she was soft spoken and graceful in her manner.

Cindy was born in 1994, when her mother was in her late thirties, and her father, Ian, had already turned forty. Because both of her parents were employed at full-time professional jobs when she was born, an unmarried older sister of her father came to live in their apartment in Hangzhou. Even though Cindy was enrolled in the nearby Zhejiang University day care/kindergarten from the age of two, her aunt continued to live with the family and to share child-care responsibilities for several years during her early childhood. In Chinese tradition, it has always been the acknowledged role of the father's parents or someone else in his extended family to assist with taking care of babies and infants. Ian's parents were both deceased by 1994, and his sister was the only female sibling available.

They lived in a small apartment in the faculty village near to the campus of Zhejiang University where Cindy's father taught English. From an early age, Cindy was drawn to books, especially ones with pictures and storybooks from both Chinese and English cultures. Her mother taught her to read before she began primary school at age six. She started the learning process with pinyin, the romanized method of writing Chinese characters. When I met her, Chinese was still her favorite school subject and she was a member of the reading club at the children's section of the provincial library.

However, by age eleven Cindy had focused her principal interest on art. As her father showered us with numerous gifts throughout the year, we received many of her creations as presents. At Christmas time she made us a jolly Merry Christmas card, as she shared in the enjoyment of the holiday along with many other urban Chinese families while at the same time overlooking its Christian significance. For the Chinese New Year, which we were invited to celebrate at their apartment, Cindy presented us with a beautifully illustrated "Happy Spring Festival" menu. She wrote out the names of the nine dishes in both cursive English and in Chinese characters and mounted the list on heavy red paper. She enclosed the menu in a hand-drawn frame of wooden twigs to which she added small pictures of mushrooms, fish in a pot and a small bird. That evening we also saw how she had decorated her bedroom with her own paintings of fashionably dressed women.

When I asked her what she wanted to be when she grew up, she replied in Chinese without hesitating, "a painter." Not only was her passion and talent for drawing readily apparent but she also indirectly enlightened me about art education in China. Earlier, I had received as a present a drawing from another eleven-year-old. He had asked me what he should draw and I had replied: "Anything you want to," expecting that he would draw a landscape or maybe a person's face. When he handed me his drawing, I was surprised to see how accurately he had copied a cartoon depiction of a boy astride a motorcycle. That was my first indication that Chinese children learned to draw by careful copying of other people's art.

A story called "A Painting of Bullfighting by Dai Song," which Cindy wrote for school and which was displayed on the bulletin board outside the provincial children's library, confirmed my earlier preconception. Her Chinese teacher had assigned the class to write an essay about a rural folk tale whose main character was a man who loved to collect calligraphy and paintings. One of his cherished possessions by a well-known artist was a painting called "Bullfighting," and according to Cindy it portrayed the bull's tail "in a nonsensical manner." "When a bull fights, his tail hangs tightly between its legs, but the bull in this painting is wiggling his tail while fighting," Cindy explained in her essay, expressing disapproval for art that was not entirely realistic. Her piece ended with a moral: "The story tells us: artistic creation must be based on true life."

Other than art Cindy had strong predilections for things female. She still liked dolls and chose books to read in both Chinese and English about princesses and romances. The clothes she wore to school were the most fashionable style of jeans and even her winter jacket was brightly-colored with decorative designs on the sleeves.

In several respects, her lifestyle illustrated changes that have taken place in recent years in Chinese society. The food she ate and especially savored reflected her mother's strongly health-conscious attitudes. She enjoyed tangerines and would eat them instead of candy and ordered yoghurt as her drink at a restaurant. Because her mother was a physician the family was particularly attuned to cleanliness and avoided eating at popular nearby restaurants. Cindy liked to help her mother in the kitchen and made sure that we were aware that she had prepared the assorted fruit dish for our Spring Festival feast.

Her best friend was a classmate who wanted to be a backpacker when she grew up. When I asked her how she thought that she would earn a living, she immediately responded that she would work half the year and travel the other half. Cindy had learned to swim during the previous summer, having taken lessons at the university's outdoor swimming pool. When my husband and I had visited that pool, we had noticed that very few people of our age could be seen in the deep water. A retired mathematics professor, whom we met in the shallow end of the pool, was astonished that I knew how to swim. "When I was a child, we didn't have a chance to learn how to swim," he bemoaned.

On the other hand, in many ways Cindy seemed like a traditional child. She did not appear to crave independence; on the contrary, she rode on the back of her father's bicycle, and Ian admitted that he had not yet taught her to ride a bike because of concerns about road safety. She was afraid of dogs, even though many urban Chinese are nowadays acquiring pets as status symbols. When we visited a historical tourist village with

Ian and his daughter, she chose to lead us to a performance of a shadow play, a traditional type of theater that involved the artful manipulation of puppets made with many movable parts.

Later, when we toured the Taoist temple in this village, I detected for the first time a generational conflict between father and daughter. Cindy was fascinated by the ritual in the temple, and went directly to the statue of her animal zodiac sign. When she got into a long line to have her fortune told by a Taoist practitioner, her father somewhat abruptly announced that it was time to leave the temple. He confessed, "I don't really approve of this hokus pocus as I grew up in Mao's China."

Weiqiu

Weiqiu, who was born in 1998, is the cousin of one of the rural students described in chapter 2. I met her when I visited Fan Gao's home in Anhui province. She is the second-born child of Fan Gao's aunt and uncle, who operate a private pharmacy in the small town of Sankou. Even though governmental policy in China forbids two-children families, this rural couple was able to pay a substantial fee of 10,000 *yuan* ($1250) in order to have their daughter. Her older brother, who was born in 1986, is now about to leave home to begin his studies at university. He will attend Anhui Normal University, where he will study to become a primary school teacher.

When I arrived in Sankou with Fan Gao after our eight-hour bus trip from Hangzhou, Weiqiu greeted us alongside her parents and older brother in the front room of their house, which is a drugstore. Fan Gao playfully lifted his young cousin into the air. After we had enjoyed a drink we were ushered through the shop into the family's living room. We sat on the sofa while Weiqiu, a tall, cute seven year old who was missing her two front teeth, seated herself at a synthesizer keyboard and played several tunes for me. She had been taking lessons for one year and could read music written with do/re/mi notations. Here was my introduction to rural China: a child playing a Western instrument and reading Western music.

Weiqiu continued to astonish me throughout my three-day visit. Every time I saw her she was wearing the same white cotton frock full of frills that her mother had just bought for her at a shop in the nearby bigger town. She liked this dress so much that, during the day I climbed Yellow Mountain with her brother and older cousins, her mother had washed it and ironed it so that she could wear it again in the evening.

She fit the designation of pampered that the media continually complain about. Not only did she have toys, books, and all the food she desired to eat, but she also lacked discipline. While her parents both worked as pharmacists, Weiqiu ran around the house and shouted whenever she wanted something. Her mother did all the cooking and household cleaning and her father plucked the feathers off the duck for the evening meal, caught fish, cared for the dog and did the grocery shopping, while her grandmother washed up the dishes after every meal. She was quickly bored and would attempt to climb ladders or get into mischief without being reprimanded. Aware that she was a cute girl, she was able easily to direct the attention of her parents, aunts, uncles or cousins to herself.

On the other hand, she is able to reap the benefits that are emerging for her generation. She enjoys reading books, singing, watching television, and playing with a cousin four years older than she. She rides her own bicycle and sits on the back of her uncle's motorcycle. Even though she is growing up in a small rural town, she has already seen much more of China than her older brother, for she has accompanied her parents on their holiday travels by bus and train.

Primary School

I visited four primary schools during my year in China, but only at the Affiliated Primary School of Zhejiang University was I able to meet students and teachers and become acquainted with textbooks and the curriculum. This primary school, which was built in 1957, is one of the key schools established by the Chinese Ministry of Education in the late 1970s as models for others to emulate. These schools also have the most modern facilities and the best-trained teachers. In other respects, however, key schools are not noticeably different from all other 366,200 primary schools (2005 statistics, *China Daily* online, August 8, 2006).

All the urban primary schools that I toured were larger establishments than I was used to seeing in the United States and in western Europe. This one consisted of several four- and five-story buildings constructed in a U-shape, with a metal gate at the entrance way. In the center of the U-space was a huge, tiled area where children played games during recess and lined up before leaving school at 4 o'clock every afternoon. Along one side of the buildings lay the playing field, running track and basketball court. Atop the main school building stood a sculpture of an eagle and beside it a red Chinese flag waved upon a flagpole. On my tour of the school, I was shown the library, gymnasium, computer room, art room, multipurpose room, and teachers' offices, and was told that this school lacked a cafeteria. There is a kitchen but the children eat their lunches in their classrooms.

There were 1452 students at this school, divided into six grades, with approximately fifty students in each class and five classes per grade level. Chinese children begin grade one at the age of six years, and in the sixth-grade English class that I taught the students were either eleven or twelve years old. The primary school curriculum includes Chinese and mathematics in each grade, as well as fine arts, music, moral character, physical education and science. In grade three English language study begins as well as some type of social studies instruction, such as geography, Chinese history or local history. At this primary school students started instruction in the use of computers in grade three. In concert with recent reforms that emphasize "quality-oriented education," children participate in interest groups, such as music, handicraft, and drama, every Tuesday afternoon.

I knew when I had reached the English wing of the school in which I was to teach a forty-five minute English lesson, because the school motto decorating the back wall of the classroom was written in English, as well as in Chinese characters, and read: Manners, Diligence, Solidarity, Initiative. The children were seated at metal desks in rows of two, one boy with one girl. Full-length windows lined both sides of the room, with large blackboards on the front and back walls. I hung up a map of the United States next to the teacher's desk on the front blackboard and began my lesson with an introduction of myself. I passed around photographs of my house in Vermont and of my mother, husband, grown daughter and her husband.

The appearance of the students was somewhat surprising, for they were taller and huskier than I had expected for a class of eleven-year-olds. Their clothing varied enormously from child to child, with several girls wearing fashionably tailored sweaters and boys in checkered sweaters or sweatshirts. Many wore school jackets with red Young Pioneer scarves draped around their necks. An unusually large proportion of children wore eyeglasses, as did the young English teacher who was dressed in a jeans jacket and long pants.

These sixth-graders had been studying English since grade three, and judging from the level of their textbook they had acquired basic conversational competence. In order to prepare my lesson for that day the English teacher had loaned me a copy of the class textbook. *PEP Primary English Students' Book* was published in 2003 by Beijing's Lingo Media and People's Education Press, and was a joint Canada-China publication with assistance from the Canadian International Development Agency. There were six units in the book: "How Do You Go There?" "Where Is the Science Museum?" "What Are You Going to Do?" "I have a Pen Pal." "What Does She Do?" "The Story of Rain." For each unit the book offered chants, cartoons, stories, picture exercises, group work, reading passages, talking and pronunciation aids, songs and games. Before meeting the students I thought that this textbook appeared to be unusually advanced for sixth-graders, with information about taking the subway in Paris and paying a 15-dollar fine for jaywalking in a Canadian town.

Halfway through my period of teaching I became convinced that these students in fact had acquired a substantial knowledge of English. After a brief lesson in map reading, I pointed to the northern border of the United States. "What is the name of that country?" I asked the class. I heard several shouts of "Canada." Various students recognized the cities of New York and Seattle on the map, but no one had ever heard of my state: Vermont. To illustrate I showed the class pictures of a red dairy barn, fall foliage, a white-steeple church, and a snowy mountain scene from a "Beautiful Vermont Calendar."

Then I shifted positions, responding to their questioning of me. One girl stood up and asked how old I was. Then a boy wanted to know how many members were in my family and another the date of my birthday. One boy wondered whether I thought Hangzhou was beautiful and another asked me what I did on Sundays. Naturally, several were curious about my favorite things. One girl asked which was my favorite food and another which was my favorite season. Not only were these Chinese sixth-graders inquisitive, but they were also exuberant, well-informed about the world, and enthusiastic about playing games and singing songs in English. We

162

tried out "Simon Says" until things got a bit rowdy and then turned to the Pete Seeger songbook from which I had photocopied "This Land Is Your Land" and "Oh, Susanna."

Junior Middle School

When I visited a seventh-grade class I found the children there to be more subdued and the atmosphere more constricting. After all, students at Daguan Middle School were already being introduced to the examination-oriented regimen of Chinese secondary education. At this urban school located in northwest Hangzhou, 1370 students attend three years of junior middle school. Although this school is not a key one, students who are successful in their studies can take an examination in their third year to enter an academic senior school that will lead to a university education. Otherwise, after the completion of this course of studies, students will either terminate their nine years of compulsory education or continue to study at a vocational high school.

The white buildings that house the school are quite similar in architectural style to those of the primary school. They rise several stories high and the classrooms are connected to each other by open corridors that face onto a tiled yard. Classrooms are furnished with the requisite technological equipment of computers, overhead projector, and screen, and the students sit in twos at the same type of metal desks with wooden tabletops that open up into drawers. Missing from this lower secondary school classroom was the motivational school motto that decorated the back wall of the primary school. Instead, the white-painted wall was left blank. In the corner stood one space heater, but its force, if it were in fact turned on, was not strong enough to warm up the large classroom. Students sat in class dressed in their school uniform jackets, and I wore my coat. One of the teachers wore red woolen gloves, which led her students to call her Santa Claus, she mentioned to me.

Daguan Middle School comprises two teaching buildings, one newer than the other. I walked up the stairs to the fifth floor of the older building to teach an English class to seventh-graders, who had just begun their lower secondary school education. In comparison with the list of courses for primary school, their curriculum does not appear to differ markedly in content. They take the same number of classes, but now mathematics includes both geometry and algebra and the science course focuses on biology. Politics, or the study of socialist ideology, has replaced the class in moral character. Besides those curricular changes, students at junior middle school have to accustom themselves to an increase in the amount of homework assigned as well as to more challenging course work.

In addition, the content covered in each course is geared directly to a standardized national syllabus. For example, in the English-language course the lesson schedule is so tight that teachers told me they have no time to introduce supplementary material beyond what was already presented in the textbook. I appreciated their predicament. Before my visit to the junior middle school I had received a package sent to my apartment with two pages cut out of the book from Unit 9, called "Do you want to go to a movie?" Pages 54 and 55 centered around the seventh-graders' comprehension of four types of movies: comedies, action movies, documentaries, and thrillers. Also included was a section on grammar as well as a game to play in the classroom. The teachers criticized this textbook as being too difficult for children with only four years of English, with the introduction of too many new vocabulary words in each lesson. I agreed.

I started off my English class with a brief personal introduction and display of the USA map, and then went immediately into the assignment for the day. I asked the class to name examples of the four types of films. They came up with *Home Alone* for a comedy; *Harry Potter* for a thriller; *Shaolin* for an action movie; and a film about Deng Xiaoping, who was the former leader of China, for a documentary. This was a hard-going exercise for the class and their English teacher often came to their rescue. Surprising to me was the proclivity of the class to speak in unison, repeating aloud a sentence that I had said. The grammar focus proved to be easy, replying to questions with "I do/I don't" and "She does /She doesn't."

At last came the time for playing games, when I was able to go beyond the lesson plan after completing the first game that was prescribed in the book. We polled the class, finding out how many students liked each category of film; they raised their hands to show whether they preferred comedy, thriller, action or documentary movies. The next game we played was called "Find Someone in the Class." A student stood up at the desk and queried his or her classmates: "Who likes chocolate?" The student who responded then stood up and asked another question, such as "Who has a pet?" This went on for some time, revealing that the students had already acquired a substantial English vocabulary.

But these junior middle school students were not as curious as the sixth-graders. When I opened up the class to questioning me, only one student could think of anything to ask me. "How many children do I have?" he asked. I replied that I had one daughter, and then we turned to singing English-language songs.

After teaching my classes, I was ushered into a roundtable discussion with the twenty-one English teachers at the school. Twenty were women, with a sole male teacher among the group, and all had graduated from Hangzhou Teachers College. They ranged in age from the head teacher, who had been teaching for twenty years, to young, recent graduates. Everyone had questions for me because I was a "foreign expert."

There was a barrage of questions about class participation and encouraging students to speak English: How do you teach oral English? How do you get all students to participate in group work? Do I have any suggestions about teaching vocabulary? They also asked whether I thought grammar was important to teach at junior middle school, and more generally someone wanted to know which age I thought was the best one for learning a second language.

Deqing Vocational School

After completion of junior middle school, children in China, who are customarily fifteen years old, face a decision about their next stage of education. Senior secondary schools offer academic instruction that leads to entry into institutions of higher education; vocational schools teach adolescents skills that are geared directly for the labor market. Since the 1980s, China has established a large number of vocational secondary schools that provide both job training programs and continued liberal education for approximately 7.5 million students (statistics from *China Daily* online, August 27, 2006). These schools are preparing skilled workers for jobs in such fields as finance, accounting, automobile and aircraft construction, computers, and tourism. Deqing Vocational School comprises two sections: one for vocational training and the other for liberal arts studies. I taught an English class, which is a required course for both sections.

Deqing is the main town of a county in Zhejiang province that lies approximately fourteen miles to the north of Hangzhou. It is not a large town, with only 57,000 residents, but as is commonplace in Zhejiang province, construction of new buildings can be seen everywhere. In downtown Deqing new hotels, office and apartment buildings, and a central park were all at various stages of completion.

The school grounds, situated a few miles outside of the town, spread out over a spacious campus that includes student dormitories, teaching buildings, library and athletic facilities. At the entrance, the welcoming slogan "Embrace the Future" is displayed in front of a bold steel sculpture of a globe enclosed in a spiral. It is surrounded by flower beds and backed up by three flags hoisted on flagpoles. The six-story administrative building, decorated with white walls and high ceiling, marble staircase and tiled floor, showcases a world map mounted between monumental-sized, traditional Chinese vases.

Students in the English class that I taught at this school were much more fluent in the language than were the children at either the primary or junior middle school, for by the time they entered this level of secondary education they had studied English for at least five years. This allowed for more interaction between myself and the students, who were between the ages of fifteen and seventeen. The school is coeducational, but the students sat at desks in pairs of boys or girls. Because students board at the school and because the students are teenagers, there are strict regulations about socializing among the sexes. Dating is discouraged. The students spoke in English about liking pop culture, especially rock music, and mentioned the names of their favorite stars. They told me that they enjoyed eating pizza and playing sports. When I showed a photograph of my mother, who was 85, I asked whether any student had such an elderly relative. No one had, although two mentioned grandparents who were in their seventies. Most said that they were the only child in their family.

Although I received a copy of the English textbook, I was free to base my lesson on my own material. Chinese educators consider it worthwhile for students, who are being trained to enter the workforce, to be exposed to native speakers of English. Everyone realizes that in a globalized market knowledge of foreign languages is a necessity. Some of the students I met that day were training to be flight attendants and others were preparing to cook in restaurants.

Their textbook, *Senior English for China Student's Book 1B,* was published in 2003 by the People's Education Press in Beijing. The ten units in the book deal with contemporary issues, drawing on a mixture of Chinese and international examples. The unit "Scientists at work" encourages students to discuss and to write about advantages and disadvantages of various scientific discoveries and applications. The particular technology featured is Shanghai's high-speed Maglev (magnetic levitation) train. The text includes a sample debate that introduces contentious points, such as its considerable expense and its positive impact on the environment. Another topic raised in this unit is the use of animals for scientific experimentation, with the viewpoint of animal rights activists presented in the reading assignment. On the other hand, the unit on "Modern agriculture" describes only the positive effects of genetically modified crops, emphasizing how this technique could help China compensate for its severe shortage of arable land. In addition to these informational topics, there were units on "Humour," "Body language" and "A world of fun."

While playing interactive games in the classroom, students revealed their knowledge of both world geography and travel. Their English vocabularies were extensive. When they stood up to answer questions or to participate in word games, they were less hesitant and more comfortable with the language compared to younger Chinese students whom I had taught.

In the middle of the class period a bell rang to signify the onset of a daily activity that I learned was widespread throughout Chinese schools. For ten minutes students engaged in exercises to strengthen their eyes. Educators had initiated these exercises twenty-five years ago in response to a noticeable deterioration in the eyesight of Chinese children, but a large proportion of students continue to need to wear eyeglasses. In my conversations with several educational officials I was assured, however, that these eye exercises were having some impact on correcting the condition.

Chinese Schools

Even though I taught English classes at each level of Chinese schools: kindergarten, primary, junior middle, and vocational secondary school, essays written by my university students about their school days offer additional insights into China's educational system. These students, who were born in the 1980s, had attended primary and junior middle school during the 1990s, while their three years of senior secondary school education took place in the twenty-first century. The best description was written by an "A" student from Guangdong province.

> As the products of the Chinese educational system, we know what the rest of the world would think of us: victims of rote-learning, unimaginative bookworms, silent listeners to lectures, and uncreative exam-takers. We would fight to protect our reputation, but unfortunately there is an element of truth in these stereotypes.
>
> China's public education, deep-rooted in the theories of Confucianism, has been undergoing incessant reforms and improvement, but China's education still has a long way to go to catch up with the international advanced level. One of the main problems is that China's education remains exam-oriented.
>
> In ancient China, there was a stratifying examination system for the purpose of selecting virtuous and wise persons to assist the emperor in ruling the nation. Today, passing exams may not necessarily launch you on a political career, but the significance has not diminished. Exams can save us a lot of decision-making, for they determine what schools we are going to, what jobs we can get, and even what life we are expecting. In order to excel in life, we have to excel in exams first. This is understandable, though. In such a vast country with shrinking resources and a swelling population, the distribution of wealth requires certain mechanisms to avoid disorder. The exam system, as one of the mechanisms, at least offers a relatively fair tool for competition.
>
> Therefore, Chinese students, having been repeatedly indoctrinated with the "law of the jungle" from early childhood, participate in the marathon of examinations, conscientiously or reluctantly. While our foreign counterparts might be happily catching butterflies or racing with the wind, we Chinese whiz kids are already reciting Tang poems or solving equations. Endless homework squeezes amusement out of our schedules. Teachers and parents are zealously involved. But instead of arousing curiosity, cultivating interest and stimulating thoughts, all they can do is to offer children more efficient ways to pass exams with flying colors. Some creative teachers would like to adorn their classes with interesting activities, but if they do so, they would fall behind with the compact and overloaded syllabus. A usual class consists of the teacher's explaining and the students' note-taking. Fun is a luxury.
>
> The national college entrance examination, as one of the most important exams in China's educational system, is a ruthless sieve. The happy few come through; others don't. But for high school students who have been in the crucible of physical and mental ordeals

for so many years, this big exam somehow signals the light at the end of the tunnel. College has always been described as heaven, in contrast to the hell of high school, and this exam bridges hell and heaven. Now that I am a junior in Zhejiang University, it turns out that college is not heaven, but at least it is life. The pressure of exams still exists, but we have more stretching space. Once in college, we are like bewildered birds, suddenly let loose after years of captivity. Some get lost, not knowing where to go; while others run riot, thinking it high time to compensate for lost pleasure.

There is a chain in a child's education, from kindergarten on, to primary school, middle school, college, or even higher. Each step of education should accommodate the progressive development of the young minds. But China's education system seems to be going the other way around, all because of exams. If the priority is not shifted from the testing of learning to learning itself, China's educational system should be renamed examination system. After all, education is an important examination that the Chinese government cannot afford to flunk.

What most university students remembered about primary school was a less-pressurized atmosphere than they experienced at later stages in their schooling. As one student phrased it, "Life in the primary school was much happier and funnier with more leisure." However, for another young woman who wrote a personal essay with the title "Score Is Not Everything," her striving for high test results began when she was a pupil in grade four. She wrote:

One afternoon when school was over, everyone went home as usual except me. Why? Because I received my test paper and got a rather bad result which was beyond my belief, and I was sure, beyond my parent's too. What's worse, my teacher had asked me to have my parent's signature on it and hand it in. I wandered in the street with no directions, in fear and trembling, worrying about what was waiting for me. I dared not raise my head because even a casual look of the passers-by was like a fierce sword to me, as if they knew about my shameful score and were ready to laugh at me.

When I reached home, it was already half an hour later than my usual time. Luckily, neither of my parents was at home, which meant that I still had time to think about my excuses. At that time, there was a familiar laughter coming from the neighborhood. Suddenly an idea flashed to my mind — I could get my neighbor's signature instead and she would help me to keep this secret. So I ran to the door at once, with the paper in my hand. Things always go against our imagination. Just the moment I opened the door, I found my mother standing there, ready to unlock it. What a surprise! My heart leapt and immediately I hid my paper on the back. "Where are you going?" asked my mother. "I ... I'm going to the rubbish," I answered in quite a low voice, feeling my face incarnadined, although I could not see it. "Then where is the rubbish and what's on your hand?"

Of course, I didn't carry out my plan, but to my surprise I wasn't blamed as I expected either. Instead, I was told to correct my mistakes on the paper and not to make the same mistakes any longer. I am thankful for having such understanding and enlightened parents who don't regard the score as everything.

Another student remembered an entirely different experience. She wrote in her essay: "During the first two years in primary school, we immersed ourselves with songs and dances. It's amazing that we loved chasing each other during breaks so much. The whole school was filled with shouting and laughing." But then she went on to report on the disciplined atmosphere in the classroom:

We typically started the day with a greeting dialogue:

TEACHER: Class begins.

MONITOR: Stand up!

TEACHER: Good morning students.

STUDENTS: Good morning teacher.

Every student was required to sit up straight and put one forearm over the other. Most importantly, we should listen carefully and quietly to what the teacher said. In every class, the teacher was the most powerful person, may I say so, for no one dared to disobey his or her requirement. We were so obedient that no one would argue with the teacher.

We had about 45 students in each classroom, who were divided into eight groups according to our statures, and each group had one group leader whose duty was to collect students' homework and hand it in or help the teacher check that each one of the group members could recite the texts required.

Above the group leader were course representatives, students who did an excellent job in the course. I used to be the Chinese representative, for the teacher in charge of my class thought my Chinese was better than most other students. Though much honored, I was responsible to hand in and out my classmates' exercise books; moreover, I should lead the morning reading before classes every day. Other representatives for the courses like math, P.E. and science had their own duties. All the group leaders, cadres and monitors had a cloth badge, though with different ranks, which we wore on our left arm whenever we went to school.

A few essay writers tried to pinpoint the contrast between primary school and junior middle school. One student wrote: "Junior middle school students are less active and brisk. Students always are quiet in the class and there are less ask-and-answers." Another student compared two teachers she had for Chinese lessons, one from primary school and the other from middle school. She wrote:

> It was in grade 5 in elementary school that my Chinese course performance reached its crest, and I owe it to the teacher who taught me at that time. She was a really competent teacher. She not only taught me the knowledge but also a lot of other things which interested me, like composition. She told us that if we wanted to write out a good article, careful observation was very necessary because materials always came from lives, besides reading a lot of books. So when I met the teacher who taught me Chinese in middle school, my performance became awful quickly. He just wanted us to make good marks so that other people would consider him as a good teacher. He required us to recite texts according to examinations. I was totally annoyed by these assignments so that my enthusiasm for Chinese disappeared.

"Dull," "hard," and even "desperate" were how most university students described senior high school, which lasted for three years after the completion of junior middle school. Their priority was preparing for the National College Entrance Examination, which turned out to be their entrée into Zhejiang University. Some students cherished happy memories from this time period; one titled his essay "Bitter Happiness."

> My heart goes back to the years when the National College Entrance Examination is the thick cloud covering the crescent moon in every student's mind. Entering a good university was almost all that I strove for. Everything seemed to have been designed and all I have to do was memorizing, following and obeying. My teachers often talked through the whole class and we were there to listen.
> Sometimes sitting on the grass, looking straight up at the sky, I know that it was a fine afternoon, to be sure, with a clear sky, warm sunshine and a gentle breeze. But that had nothing to do with me. Due to the monotonous life, in which I had class after class, paper

after paper, and hurrying on the campus without enough rest, I am often tired. My energy and enthusiasm had been squeezed out of my body. My creativity and ingenuity had been driven out of my brain. I had little time to enjoy my hobbies; I had little time to think of the meaning of life. The gloomy life might be a like a tranquil lake, but the water was dead. It was not my home.

But every coin has two sides. After the dull life, I realized that there was no plain way to success. Only after pains, we would gain. I not only studied for myself but also to shoulder the responsibility for my family and society. Although the National College Entrance Examination was not the final destination of my life, it really pushed me forward.

After striving for a common goal for three years with my teachers and friends, they have become an important part in my life which will never fade in my memory. The encouragement and advice from them enlightened me like warm sunshine in spring. It was a journey from naivety to maturation. I miss it very much. In college, I am exactly like a baby who has just been weaned from its mother. I need to stop crying, learn to study and to accommodate.

Another student's essay detailed the specific regimen of high school life at a boarding school:

Everyday we were busy. We got up at about 5:15, and at 5:30 we were supposed to assemble at the playground to run 800 meters, which probably was the only exercise for most students in the day. After the running, we began our morning reading class, in which everybody read loudly to memorize or recite something. The whole day was full of classes: we had five classes in the morning and three in the afternoon. We had to learn many subjects: Chinese, mathematics, English, physics, chemistry, biology, history, geography, politics. In the evening, there were still self-learning classes that ended at 9:00. We only had a half-day off each week and two days off each month. Almost all of our time, except sleeping and eating, was used for studying. At grade three, each month we would take a simulative exam, copying the form and timing of the final real entrance examination.

The studying was bitter, but there was also something sweet — the friendship among classmates. We tackled problems together, relaxed together, we dreamed about the university life together. Together, we walked through that hard time.

Compulsory education in China extends for nine years and includes six years of primary school and three years of junior middle school. This has been governmental policy since the introduction of the Law on

Compulsory Education in 1986. Nonetheless, at the present time even this limited extent of schooling is not available to all Chinese children. A university student from Zhejiang province wrote:

> In my hometown the case is that every child can have the opportunity to accept the nine-year compulsory education nowadays. But as I learn more about the outside world, I find that the situation in many places is rather poor. Once I watched a TV program about the education in the mountain areas in China on CCTV. From that, I really realized the backwardness in the mountain areas in China. In that program, I saw the students study in a so-called classroom without any desks, chairs and a blackboard. And the textbooks they used were borrowed from others by their teachers. Besides, many of the students had to walk quite a long distance to attend classes. Still many children could not go to school because of the economical difficulty of their family. Much to people's surprise, many of them did not know what a computer was. Looking at the expression in their eyes, we can clearly read their aspiration for knowledge which was quite difficult to acquire for them.

An idealistic university student wrote in her essay entitled "The wave of graduate-volunteers pouring into western China" about a small step that is being taken to balance the educational situation between the prosperous east coast and the poor towns and villages of twelve western provinces in China:

> It's summer again. College graduates are making a significant choice in their life: to work or to further study. Some would be busy with job-hunting, while others may go into the hard process of preparing for their postgraduate entrance examination. But now a third group has emerged: they are preparing for their serving in West China, working as volunteers to promote the growth of the western poor areas. They are all answerers to the call of a scheme announced by our government two years ago. The planned number of volunteers has increased from 5,000 in 2003 to 11,300 in 2005.
>
> Education must be placed on our development agenda as a strategic priority, in which large numbers of intellectuals are badly needed. However, the reality is that the poorer the area is, the fewer the intellectuals are. So it's imperative to introduce intellectuals from the east. Transferring a part of freshly graduated college students to the west is an advisable and necessary action with multiple benefits, which could not only help prosper the west, but also relieve the stresses and strains of the job market as well as enrich the lives of those volunteers and improve their work abilities.

7

Conclusion

The thirteen Chinese students and teachers featured in this book have all been witness to the changes — sometimes turbulent, sometimes calm — that have transformed Chinese society since 1949. Which societal transformation they happened to experience has depended largely upon their decade of birth. Personal biographies of teachers, who were born in the 1950s, 1960s or 1970s, varied enormously from those of university students who were born in the 1980s, and from children who were born in the 1990s.

One way to appreciate these vast differences is to compare attitudes toward communist ideology and life values among the five generations. Ian, who was born in the 1950s, was schooled in the thought of Mao Zedong and came of age during the Cultural Revolution. When China opened up to the world in the 1980s he had the opportunity to study in England, where he perfected his academic expertise but also remembered his visit to Karl Marx's tomb as one of the highlights from his year abroad. Professor Chen, who was born in the 1960s, although raised under the influence of communist ideology found her calling in life as a scientist only in the 1980s and 1990s when Chinese society began to encourage individual aspirations. Shirley, Shao Bin, and Alice, all born in the 1970s, represent the transitional generation, when China started to move away from a planned economy toward a market orientation. Their schooling during the 1980s combined elements from Mao's China with reform ideas of Deng

174

Xiaoping, and as adults they have often been caught between the two worlds. They may retain communist notions of selfless dedication to serving the interests of the Chinese people, but in order to prosper in their careers they face the competitive atmosphere of contemporary China.

The post-opening up generation, those born in the 1980s and 1990s, have known only a market-oriented economy and have accepted communist teachings in school with a large dose of skepticism. Many university students do not see any relevance in the politics courses that they have been taught from junior middle school through postgraduate studies. Some continue to respect and believe in communist ideals but cannot relate those values to China's present society. Others are exploring alternatives such as Confucianism, Christianity or Buddhism. Some have accepted consumer attitudes while others scorn Western cultural influences, ambivalent about what they actually believe in amidst so many choices.

Yet, in the twenty-first century they all are participants in forging the next face of China, creating a future Chinese society that will build upon the historical events of the last five decades, but will differ markedly from the past as well. In 2005, the country was making preparations to launch its 11th Five Year Plan for the years from 2006 to 2010, which promises not only to continue a modernization drive of almost thirty years' duration but also foresees radical changes in the offing. Instead of an all-out concentration on economic growth as heretofore, the future goal is to ensure common prosperity, closing the glaring gaps in living conditions among various segments of the Chinese population.

China in the twenty-first century is a dynamic society that attracts visitors, students, businessmen and people from all over the world desirous of participating in the creation of this new world. On my last day in Hangzhou, I guided a young couple who had just arrived from Beijing to a hotel. Both were in their twenties: the man was from Benin in Africa and was studying for a doctorate in international relations at Renmin University; the woman, a student of Chinese language, was from Zurich in Switzerland. I asked them why they had come to China. The young Swiss woman replied effusively: "Here I can act and study and live the way I want to. I have never felt so free in my life."

I was quite taken aback by her response. Imagine China as more free than a western European country! Then I remembered the sentiments expressed in the five-minute speeches that my second-year university students had presented: "Being cool is being yourself, using your own talents"; "The way to be optimistic: write down three things that make you happy everyday"; "Success needs a treacherous path to overcome"; "Education is self-development"; "Are we losing Chinese traditional values? No, now we export our values"; "Old nation with new life."

The new face of Chinese culture is almost as striking as the new faces of the people and the economy. Not only are the Internet and short-text messages on cell phones transforming the ways people are communicating, but also popular music, theater, and films are merging Chinese traditions with global trends. Korean soap operas flood the television channels and Japanese cartoons are children's favorites, while a singing competition called Super Girls, the Chinese version of American Idol, created a national craze. The 800 million viewers of the Spring Festival TV gala in 2006, an annual extravaganza show first broadcast in the early 1980s, watched the full range of Chinese cultural offerings: ethnic songs and dances, breakdance performances, hip-hop pop stars, traditional opera renditions of *Butterfly Lovers,* and even a song written by a migrant laborer called "Thinking of the Year I Left Home."

Building a "harmonious society" was the catchphrase in 2005 amidst a realization that imbalances within China between rich and poor, urban and rural areas, eastern and western regions were in urgent need of correction. The overriding question was how to reduce and eventually eliminate these disparities that have cropped up, especially during the past ten years. How to create an equitable situation in a China where some children spend summer holidays on school trips to Australia and others cannot afford to pay the required tuition and fees to attend high school? How to establish social justice between parents who buy medicines to guarantee a child's mental and physical comfort during the lead-up to the nerve-wracking National College Entrance Exam and the Chinese families whose limited incomes do not allow for visits to a doctor when illnesses occur? How to guarantee that technological competence is utilized to send Shenzhou VI into space and at the same time to bring electricity to remote rural villages with windmill-and-solar renewable energy systems?

There is widespread acclaim for and approval of what China has achieved in reforming its economy since 1978, but there is disapproval and open admission of failure in many aspects of its social policy reforms. However, as Norwegian researcher Jon Pedersen revealed in a 2006 publication of results from a five-year survey conducted in western China: "Compared with other developing areas in the world that I have been to, the feeling of optimism about the future that people show is the most striking" (quoted in online *China Daily,* October 4, 2006).

Professor Ezio Manzini of Milan (at Italy's polytechnic university), a foreign expert speculating about China's future direction, has been impressed by "China's amazing energy." He foresees a possibility for China to reorient itself away from "mainly quantitative growth towards qualitative, sustainable development." With the emphasis in China today on innovation and tackling environmental problems he contends: "Leapfrog strategies are a possibility for new economies to shift directly from where they are to the most advanced solutions.... China has the unique possibility to find an innovative and more sustainable solution, to produce what is needed for its internal market and, in doing so, to offer effective and economic solutions to large and global issues such as energy, mobility, healthy food and elderly care" (quoted in *China Daily*, September 8, 2006).

In China today, establishing harmony refers to solving problems, especially in the realms of health care, social security, education, environmental protection, family planning, rural development and governmental management. The hurdles as well as some of the solutions to these challenges are highlighted below. The chapter ends with the voices of future faces of Chinese society, expressed in several essays written by students in my English writing class.

Health Care

In the middle of 2005 the government made public its conclusions that its medical and public health reform had been "basically unsuccessful." According to Ge Yanfeng of the China Development Research Center, "The improper use of market mechanisms has resulted in a gross injustice in the distribution of health resources.... Lower-end health institutions, such as rural hospitals and community hospitals in urban areas, are struggling for survival" (*China Daily*, March 18, 2006). Others have pointed to the high costs of drugs and lack of health insurance as the crux of the problem. Many Chinese people seldom visit doctors or hospitals, but instead they will use whatever funds they have to buy Western and traditional Chinese medicine.

During my year in China, at least once a week the Chinese media ran a heartrending story about parents committing suicide because they were unable to afford medical care for either themselves or their families. Health-care problems impacted families interviewed in this book as well. For example, after An Xin's father suffered a debilitating injury at his construction job, the standard of living of the family decreased as a result (see chapter 3). Before the reform policies of the 1980s, China relied upon "barefoot doctors," who provided basic health care services free of charge. They were usually middle school graduates who had been trained in first aid.

The problems are legion, but no overall solution has been decided upon. In 2003 the central government began to redress the widespread lack of health insurance. It launched on a trial basis a new type of rural cooperative medical care system, which 410 million farmers had joined by the beginning of 2007. Under the system, each year a farmer contributes approximately $1 and state, provincial, municipal and county governments jointly contribute $5. Families receive partial reimbursement from the fund for medical expenses. However, according to a recent report the average rate of reimbursement has been only 26 per cent of costs incurred (*China Daily* online, March 5, 2007).

Social Security

The shifting from a centrally planned to a market economy has been a gradual process, and only in the 1990s did the Chinese government introduce the social security system that is in operation today. In the past, Chinese enterprises provided pension payments for retirees by collecting a designated sum from the salaries of the working staff. Whereas now with the institution of individual pension accounts, only a small proportion of the working population is included in China's old-age pension system, mainly those who work in the state sector.

Care of elderly parents was a concern mentioned by several of the people I interviewed. In the case of Fan Gao's parents, all siblings in the family had assumed shared responsibility for the grandmother's lodging (see chapter 2). Evelyn's grandparents continued to maintain themselves in their own apartment in Hangzhou (chapter 1).

Chinese Vice Premier Huang Ju identified the shortcomings of the present system at the first meeting of the China Social Security Forum in September 2006. He called for the development of a long-term mechanism that takes into account the particular characteristics of the Chinese labor market. Even though the financial resources of the old-age pension fund have been increasing at a rate of 20 percent annually, nevertheless the demographics of a rapidly expanding population aged 60 or above make it very difficult to maintain.

The recently uncovered social security fund scandal in Shanghai that led to the downfall of the city's leading politician has revealed the prevalence of management problems. In most Chinese cities a labor and social security bureau administers the pension fund, and there is no independent monitoring or auditing. Misuse of social security funds is widespread. Property developers who bribe government officials to finance speculative projects are only the most blatant signs of corruption. The headline-grabbing story from Shanghai that involved borrowing from the city's more than one billion dollar pension fund brought the severity of the problem into public consciousness.

Education

In 1986 the government of China passed a nine-year compulsory education law, but because of inadequate funding in 2005 significant segments of Chinese children still were unable to complete nine years of schooling. Problems with the educational system are no secret and have been written about for years. University students who had received their schooling in prosperous regions were aware of inequities in China's provision of education (see chapter 6). However, correcting the problems has been delayed because of other priorities.

Chinese prime minister Wen Jiabao explained in a speech at Harvard University in December 2003 that he had a deep personal interest in the expansion of educational opportunity among Chinese youth. "As you probably know, I'm the son of a schoolteacher. I spent my childhood [he was born in 1942] mostly in the smoke and fire of war. When Japanese aggressors drove all the people in my place to the Central Plaza [his birth-place was Tianjin], I had to huddle closely against my mother. Later on, my whole family and house were all burned up, and even the primary school that my grandpa built himself went up in flames." In March 2006 the premier confessed at a press conference in Beijing that "the problems I find most heartbreaking during my past three years' work are that I haven't been able to better solve the problems that Chinese people are most concerned about like health, education, housing and social security" (*China Daily* online, March 14, 2006).

Access to free schooling is a central issue for China and one that embarrasses its leaders. In 2005 the Chinese government devoted only 2.7 percent of its GDP to spending on education, whereas the international norm was 4 percent. By 2006 the figure had risen only marginally, to 2.82 percent of GDP. Since 1993 the government repeatedly has promised to increase spending to 4 percent but has not followed through on its promise.

China's problems with education today are closely linked to the manner in which social reforms were introduced twenty-five years ago. In the 1980s the responsibility for the administration of schools was decentralized, transferred from the central government to local governments, and in the 1990s eighty percent of the burden of financing schools was shifted to local counties and townships. A report in *China Daily* (August 22, 2005) concluded that "the county- and township-level governments have shouldered a burden that is disproportionate to their fiscal strength."

Furthermore, county and township governments that manage education at the grassroots level do not distribute funding for education equitably. Local governments divert funds designated for compulsory education to other purposes and over-invest in key and demonstration schools. They then charge parents fees in order to provide essential school services, and the poorer families who cannot afford the school fees withdraw their children from school. To counteract this type of negligence by local governments, the central government has made specific allocations for the renovation of school buildings in central and western China and for construction of rural boarding schools and distance learning projects.

In the 11th Five Year Plan, the central government has devised a schedule of actions to remedy the most basic failings in the educational system. The government intends to concentrate on three aspects of reform. It will strive to ensure access to compulsory education for all, promote vocational education, and improve the quality of higher education.

Eliminating school fees is the requisite first step to guarantee access to nine years of schooling to all Chinese children. In 2006, children in 592 key counties attended free elementary and junior middle schools. In 2007, poor children in all rural areas received free compulsory education, and by the end of 2007 Premier Wen Jiabao has pledged "completely to eliminate tuition and miscellaneous fees for all rural students." That policy will benefit 160 million school-age children who account for nearly 80 percent of the country's primary and middle school students.

The Chinese Ministry of Education in February 2007 sent a special team to nine central provinces to oversee allocation of funds for compulsory education. The team is investigating "whether students are overcharged and whether salaries of teachers engaged in compulsory education are still lower than those of local civil servants" (*China Daily* online, February 14, 2007). It is estimated that during the 11th Five Year Plan the government will increase education spending by $27.27 billion.

In addition to the government's emphasis on ensuring free compulsory schooling, another focal point in today's reform of education is a renewed push for vocational education. During various times since 1949 the Chinese government has campaigned for increased training of skilled workers, but now the movement is market driven. In journalist You Nuo's column headlined "Nation hungry for skilled workers," You Nuo mentions at least two types of skilled jobs, moulding technicians capable of computer-aided design and software programmers, both of which are in short supply in China (*China Daily*, May 6, 2005).

Students enter vocational schools after completion of their junior middle school education, and up to now these schools have been Chinese teenagers' second choice. Everyone in China wants to go to college and attendance at senior middle schools is the path to higher education. Huang Yao, who directs the Vocational and Adult Education Department at the Ministry of Education, insists that "vocational schools complement senior middle schools. We have to change the misconception that the vocational schools are inferior" (*China Daily*, October 26, 2005).

In today's China, where youth unemployment looms as a burgeoning problem, vocational schools are providing a positive alternative, especially to lower income rural families. Tuition fees for vocational schools are considerably lower than for senior middle schools, and these schools are adjusting their courses to make sure that their graduates find jobs. (See chapter 6 for a description of my visit to Deqing Vocational School in Zhejiang province.) Henan provincial authorities, for example, have established vocational unions that consist of schools, enterprises and trade associations to guarantee increased communication between schools and places of employment.

The third prong of the government's educational reform program aims to correct problems with China's system of higher education. In 1999, in response to popular demands for more places at universities, the Chinese government initiated an expanded enrollment policy for institutions of higher education. At the same time, employment practices for university graduates were reformed, with the government extricating itself from its role in the assignment of jobs. Since then, colleges and universities have seen their numbers mushroom, with 4.13 million students or approximately 21 percent of the Chinese population between the ages of 18 and 22 graduating from institutions of higher education in 2006. Before this expansion in enrollment, slightly more than one million students graduated from Chinese universities every year.

The impact of this change has affected the quality of higher education as well as employment prospects for graduates. In 2006 the Ministry of Education took action to confront both these issues. The government has agreed to restrict the growth of college enrollments and to adjust the numbers of students in accordance with local conditions. In order to combat the unemployment problem, which has resulted annually in one-quarter of graduates unable to find jobs, the government has proposed that universities and colleges adjust the curricula and majors so that more emphasis will be placed on skills training in preparation for the labor market. Also, the Chinese Communist Party's Youth League has initiated a "Serving the West Project" that sends new university graduates to work in poorer rural regions at one-tenth the salary they could earn in big cities (see student essay in chapter 6). This program has drawn out latent idealism from some recent graduates, who, in contrast to their parents who had been forced to work in the countryside during the Cultural Revolution, are choosing to volunteer to assist in regions of China that up to now have been left out of the country's economic boom.

Environmental Protection

China's environmental pollution problems are almost as famous as its economic success. According to Pan Yue, vice-minister of the State Environmental Protection Administration, "this miracle will end soon because the environment can no longer keep pace" (interview in *Der Spiegel* international online magazine, March 7, 2005). Not only is China using up too many raw materials in its unsustainable industrial development, but the country suffers from unhealthy conditions of air and water pollution as well.

In the same interview Pan Yue offered some indications of how China is attempting to protect its environment: "In some cities such as Beijing the air quality has, in fact, improved. Also, the water in some rivers and lakes is now cleaner than it's been in the past. There are more conservation areas now and some model cities that focus specifically on environmental protection. We are replanting forests. We have passed additional laws and regulations that are stricter than in the past and they are being more rigorously enforced."

Perhaps the strongest hint that the Chinese government is getting serious about combating this problem are its plans for utilizing sources of renewable energy. In the 11th Five Year Plan, the stated aim calls for 16 percent of China's power supply to come from renewable sources by 2020. Under the plan, China's major power companies are to ensure that 5 percent of their electricity generators are fuelled by renewable energy sources by 2010.

Solar and wind energy projects are operating, especially in outlying regions of China where electricity supplies from traditional grid systems have never penetrated. In a small pastoral village in far western China's Xinjiang Uygur Autonomous Region, for example, a wind-solar-diesel hybrid power system brought lights, television and computers into the community only five years ago. In northwest China's Ningxia Hui Autonomous Region nine new wind power plants are under construction, and small-scale wind-driven generators are a relatively common sight in Inner Mongolia. According to experts, wind power rather than solar power offers greater potential for expansion in China, but there are ongoing discussions with German companies interested in construction of a large-scale solar thermal power plant in Inner Mongolia.

Bio-energy has been developing rapidly in rural areas. By the end of 2005 more than 18 million peasant households were using methane gas for fuel. Large-scale coal to liquid fuel projects are underway to speed up the production of dimethyl ether, a clean-burning alternative to liquefied petroleum and natural gas.

In order to reduce its dependence on fossil fuels the Chinese government has continued to develop nuclear energy. At the present time, with nine operating reactors, nuclear power accounts for 1.6 percent of electricity output. There are plans afoot to increase nuclear power generation capacity from 8.7 million kilowatts to 40 million kilowatts by 2020 by constructing thirty additional nuclear plants. Furthermore, Chinese scientists at the Institute of Plasma Physics in Hefei, Anhui province, announced in September 2006 a successful test of an experimental thermonuclear fusion reactor, which they believe signifies a breakthrough in mankind's ability to harness a safe, clean and endless source of energy.

Solving the daunting and increasingly serious problems of water pollution will require new ways of thinking and acting, according to Tsinghua University Professor Qian Yi. "We cannot copy foreign methods in dealing with waste water," she said. The nation needs "higher efficiency and lower cost technology" (*China Daily,* September 13, 2006). The aim for the next five years is to treat 70 percent of the urban wastewater, and there are 145 wastewater treatment plants under construction in coastal areas. Measures to clean up China's waterways will focus on the polluted mouths of rivers on Bohai Bay, the Yangtze River estuary, and the lower reaches of the Pearl River delta. However, not all urban areas are located along the east coast. An Xin drew attention to the polluted river in Xianyang, her hometown, which is situated in the interior of China in Shaanxi province (see chapter 3).

With the number of car owners expected to reach 10 million by 2010 and the annual economic growth rate expected to continue to top 9 percent, prospects for reducing air and industrial pollution appear to be dim. Yet, the government is determined to enforce its environmental laws and regulations and to judge the performance of officials on how well they solve problems of the environment and society. As Pan Yue explained in the *Der Spiegel* interview, "We will close down illegal projects, including economically powerful steel, cement, aluminum and paper factories if they fail to review what effect their new investments will have on the environment."

Family Planning

In the 1970s China realized that it had a population problem. From 1949 until the early seventies the number of Chinese people had increased by approximately 300 million, which is the total population of the United States. Beginning with 550 million at the founding of the People's Republic of China, the population had reached 900 million by 1974 (Website, International Institute for Applied Systems Analysis (IIASA), Laxenburg, Austria). Because of improvements in health care, both the death rate and the infant mortality rate fell dramatically during the 1950s and 1960s while the Mao Zedong government encouraged women to procreate.

With the understanding that this continued rate of growth would neutralize future efforts to improve economic conditions, the Chinese government decided to begin to tackle the problem. In the early 1970s birth control measures were encouraged, and in 1979 China adopted a one-child policy, which required urban couples to limit births to one per family. In rural areas two children were allowed if the first child was a girl, and among ethnic minority groups no restrictions applied.

From the beginning of its application in the early 1980s until today the policy has been controversial. No one doubts, however, that it has prevented 300 million births and delayed until 2005 the growth of the population to 1.3 billion. China now belongs to a low-birth-rate list of nations with a natural growth rate of 0.9 per thousand, or an average birth rate of 1.8 children per family compared to 5.8, what it had been in the early 1970s.

All along there have been disputes about how humanely local officials have implemented the policy. A recent *Time* magazine report of "a brutal campaign of forced abortions and sterilizations" so incensed one of my students that she wrote a letter to the editor in which she accused the journalist of exaggeration and incitement. She explained that her father had been one of the administrators of the policy in Zhejiang province, and she had heard from him about the often-times fierce resistance that officials had encountered. However, the actions that the article in *Time*

(September 19, 2005) described were illegal and exceptional and portrayed the policy in a one-sided and thoroughly negative light, she wrote.

What is generally acknowledged is that China's one-child policy has led to a gender imbalance, with parents preferring boys over girls. A sample survey in 2005 showed a gender gap of 118.58:100; whereas the normal ratio is 103–107:100. This deeply rooted preference for boys in China dates back thousands of years and relates to the Confucian concept that care for parents in old age is a responsibility of male offspring.

When I discussed this issue with my interviewees I found general acceptance and support for the one-child policy. I also heard no regrets about raising a female child. Shirley, who desired a second child, was an exception among teachers whom I met (see chapter 4), whereas the parents of Weiqiu paid to have their second child (see chapter 6). University students who had grown up as only children, on the whole, expressed more criticisms. Having no siblings caused loneliness and social difficulties for some, and others felt concerned about their parents' welfare.

Another much-discussed problem that has resulted from nearly three decades of the one-child policy has been the growth of China's senior population. Demographers project that in 2010 China will have 174 million people above the age of 60, and that figure will comprise 12.78 percent of the country's total population.

In order to resolve these two problems, the Chinese government has launched a nationwide "caring for girls" campaign. In 2002 a pilot program was introduced in 24 counties where there was a serious gender imbalance. It provided annual allowances of $72 to families with no sons, when parents were over 60 years old. The Chinese government extended the policy to benefit all elderly rural families who have had no children, one child, or two daughters in 2007. Additionally, daughters who are only children are awarded bonus marks when taking the college entrance examination and their families are allowed preferential loans for agricultural production. At the same time authorities are strictly enforcing bans on the use of ultrasound equipment that determines whether a fetus is male or female, and are closing medical clinics that help to detect and abort female fetuses.

These policies are intended to alleviate the plight of rural residents who have been left out of medical insurance and social security systems. Concurrently, the program seeks to encourage young couples to adhere to the one-child policy, by assuring that in old age they will not be solely dependent upon the care provided by their children.

Rural Development

The social problem that receives the most publicity is the wide income gap between China's 750 million farmers and its 550 million urban residents. The most reliable figures report urban per capita income at between three and four times the level for rural areas. In the 1980s farmers were given a new lease on life with the introduction of the household responsibility system that rewarded those with the highest production on individually worked plots of land. Farmers' incomes rose as they applied pent-up energies to maximize agricultural output. By the 1990s, however, urban incomes began to outpace those attainable in rural areas, and the disparities have increased with the succeeding years.

The main reason that farmers have been left out of the benefits accruing from China's economic successes has been the widespread illegal practice of selling off arable land for development purposes, both industrial and residential. In southern Anhui province, in the area surrounding Yellow Mountain, farmers are losing their land for yet another purpose, burgeoning tourist development (see chapter 2). The major culprit has been identified to be local government officials who pocket the earnings from land sales, instead of adequately paying to resettle farmers and to compensate them for their crop losses. These corrupt practices have reduced China's grain harvests, allowed for extravagant investments, and pushed twenty million farmers yearly out of the countryside.

The Chinese government has taken this problem to heart, and in the 11th Five Year Plan has committed itself to build "a new socialist countryside." Specifically, this heightened emphasis means that the government will earmark funds preferentially for rural China in outlays for infrastructure, education, health care, and the environment. Premier Wen Jiabao at the beginning of 2006 announced that the government would allocate $42 billion in that year alone to rural development, approximately $6 billion more than in the previous year.

The most visible governmental action undertaken was the abolition in 2006 of the agricultural tax, removing a burden that had been levied on farmers since 1958. To compensate for the loss of tax revenue, central, provincial and city governments have allocated $12.5 billion to local governments. In addition, farmers have received direct subsidies for agricultural production. Prices paid for grain have increased, while the costs of chemical fertilizers have been controlled. Rural development advisers have encouraged regions to specialize in various cash crops: Yunnan in flowers, Xinjiang in cotton, northern China in potatoes, Fujian in poultry. More areas are growing fruit and selling herbal medicinal plants.

Not only governmental initiatives but farmers themselves are working out creative methods to close the income gap. Some have returned to the old idea of mutual help. They are setting up production-based cooperatives to pool investment and marketing, while at the same time retaining the leases for their household plots. In rural areas abutting big cities, farmers have been able to benefit from the three annual week-long national holidays that the government instituted in 1999. More and more city folk are traveling to the countryside to enjoy fresh air and food during their vacations, and rural families are hosting them at their farms.

Governmental Management

Every leader of China has tried to combat corruption, but today Hu Jintao is treating the fight against corruption as a pressing task and aims to eradicate both the symptoms and the root cause. "We are stepping up efforts to improve the rule of law and to create a culture of a clean and honest government, while strengthening the supervision of power," he pronounced in his welcoming remarks to the First Annual Conference and General Meeting of the International Association of Anti-Corruption Authorities in Beijing (online *China Daily*, October 22, 2006).

The problems have become rampant, with frequent headlines in both Chinese and international media about Chinese governmental officials losing their jobs because of corruption. The types of crimes run the gamut from bribe-taking, nepotism, illegal investments and cover-ups to widespread government-business collusion. There have been revelations of extraordinary levels of corruption in the construction and coal-mining industries, with colluding local government officials taking the major blame for China's high number of mine accidents. No region of the country has been spared. In late 2006, however, attention was directed to a number of high-profile sackings in Shanghai that involved siphoning funds for illegal investments from the city government's social security pension system.

The government has embarked on a multipronged approach to confront this scourge, relying upon the application of legal procedures and an improved selection and promotion process for senior officials. In China the 70 million members of the Communist Party manage governmental affairs to a major extent, so that combating corruption starts with reforming the behavior of Communist Party cadres. In March 2006, Hu Jintao, who is the General Secretary of the Party, released a list of "Socialist Concepts on Honor and Disgraces." These Eight do's and don'ts were heralded as a "new moral yardstick for measuring the work, conduct and attitude of Communist Party officials."

To strike at the roots of the problem, the Ministry of Education has begun to include the teaching of anticorruption in the school curriculum, aware from surveys undertaken among students that even in middle school money and position have become major temptations to children. There also has been a resurgence of interest in the study of Confucianism, which many Chinese people contend forms the foundation for the society's moral tradition.

It is too early to assess how effective any of the government's efforts have been, but one somewhat positive result can be gleaned from the latest available statistics about coal mine accidents. During 2005 nearly 6,000 people were killed in 3,341 coal mine accidents, whereas in 2006 the number of coal miners killed had been reduced to 4,746 (*China Daily* online, February 13, 2007). The major reason given for this reduction has been the closure of thousands of small, unsafe mines as a result of the crackdown on government-colliery collusion. According to the Ministry of Supervision, more than five thousand officials either in government or in state-owned enterprises have withdrawn their investments in coal mines, which in most cases provided shields for illegal operations.

The investigations into wrongdoing and the media attention accorded to this problem have heightened public awareness and have elicited positive responses. Since 2003 the National Audit Office has made public the list of governmental departments that have misused budget allocations. Thousands of Chinese Communist Party members have been expelled for corruption and taking bribes and several high-level government officials have lost their jobs. China was among the first countries to ratify the United Nations Anti-Corruption Convention, which went into effect in December 2005, and Jia Chunwang, chief of the Supreme People's Procuratorate, has been elected to chair the newly created International Association of Anti-Corruption Authorities.

Era of Hu Jintao

When Hu Jintao, president and general secretary of the Communist Party of China, visited the United States in April 2006, students and professors at Yale University heard about his expectations for his country's future. Instead of focusing solely on Deng Xiaoping's ideas for fast-track economic development, Hu Jintao's priorities for the future involve social justice, equitable distribution, and peaceful interactions based on mutual respect and the rule of law. His methods for realizing these priorities include diverting China's wealth to benefit society's have-nots, making more effective use of central governmental authority, communicating with the public in a more transparent and open manner, and basing China's forward movement on a policy that he calls "peaceful rise." These objectives of the leader are founded upon principles and attitudes that are rooted in his past.

Hu Jintao was born on December 21, 1942, in Jiangsu province. As a student in high school he was active in the Communist Youth League, and at the age of twenty-two in 1964 he joined the Communist Party of China (CCP) during his final year as a student of hydraulic engineering at Tsinghua University. His wife, Liu Yongqing, who is two years his senior, also graduated from Tsinghua University as an engineer, and both their son and daughter are Tsinghua graduates as well.

After his graduation, Hu was assigned to work at a hydropower station in northwestern Gansu province, where he advanced from engineer at the Sinohydro Engineering Bureau No. 4 to administrative positions in the province's construction department. In 1980 he was promoted to deputy director of Gansu's Ministry of Construction.

His political career dates from 1981, when he was sent to Beijing for training at the Central Party School and met the daughter of Deng

Xiaoping as well as the son of Hu Yaobang, who was general secretary of the CCP. Afterwards, Hu was appointed to a number of leadership posts in the Chinese Communist Youth League, rising to general secretary in 1984. From 1985 until 1992 he was, at first, provincial governor for three years in southwestern Guizhou province and then served for four years as Communist Party chief in the Tibet Autonomous Region.

In 1992, when he was 50 years old, he was chosen to serve on the Politburo Standing Committee, the party's highest grouping. He was by far the youngest member of the committee at the time when Deng Xiaoping still exerted strong influence and Jiang Zemin was the country's president.

Jiang Zemin chose Hu for state vice president in March 1998, assigning him to chair important task forces, to meet foreign leaders, and to serve as president of the Central Party School. To crack down on corruption among government officials, in 1999 Hu managed the Communist Party's "Three Stresses" (i.e., "stress study, stress politics, stress health trends") campaign, a professional education program with day-long sessions on ideology and morality.

He also was appointed in 1999 as vice chairman of the Central Military Commission, a position that was of crucial importance for Hu Jintao's preparation for eventual assumption of the prime responsibility. Neither Jiang Zemin nor Hu Jintao ever served in China's armed forces.

Hu Jintao's accession to general secretary of the Communist Party of China took place in November 2002, and a few months later Hu replaced Jiang Zemin as president of the People's Republic of China at the Party Congress in March 2003. Only in September 2004 did he become chairman of the Central Military Commission as well.

After reading facts about his biography and background, the question still remains: why was Hu Jintao chosen out of more than 1.3 billion people to lead China in the twenty-first century? According to Robert Lawrence Kuhn, the American author of *The Man Who Changed China: The Life and Legacy of Jiang Zemin*, which has become a bestseller in China, "President Hu has all the markings of the right leader at the right time" (New York: Crown Publishers, 2004, p. 577). Hu Jintao may not be charismatic, but Kuhn lists eight personal qualities that distinguish him: modest, honest, methodical, respectful, dedicated, telegenic, intelligent with a near-flawless memory, and close-to-the masses feeling.

But even in the "era of Hu Jintao," his face is only one among more than a billion faces of China. Hu concluded his speech at Yale University in April 2006 with a few remarks about university students: "Young people represent the hope and future of the world as they are full of vitality, new ideas and creativity. According to an old Chinese saying, 'As in the Yangtze River where the waves behind drive on those before, so a new generation always excels the last one.' I sincerely hope that the young people in China and the United States will join hands and work to enhance friendship between our two peoples, and together with people of other countries, create a better world for all."

China's Future According to the New Generation

In 2005, I taught English to hundreds of Chinese university students. These four essays that were handed in as assignments for my Advanced English writing class make me feel confident that the future of China will be in good hands.

The Chinese Dream

"Chinese Dream" is never as famous as "American Dream." Even Chinese people themselves seldom mention it. It is partly because the Chinese culture is introverted while the American culture is extroverted. However, the biggest obstacle to the spread of the concept of "Chinese dream" is that there is no clear definition of "Chinese dream."

Different from America, China has a long history. Five thousand years up and down brings about the variety of ideas and values. Truly, as other peoples on the Earth, Chinese people have their own dreams deeply rooted in heart. But the Chinese dream is in a constant change.

In ancient times, most Chinese were peasants who spent all their life in the field and were finally toiled to death. They had no dreams. The only thing they prayed for was a good rain in the spring, which was of vital importance to the harvest. They would be satisfied with themselves if they could achieve three goals in their life: having something to eat, getting married and having a son to pass down the family name. These could not be called "dreams," for they were actually the basic things of all living creatures: survival and reproduction.

The Chinese dream at that time, in my opinion, comes from the middle class. They had some education and knew the values of that time. They had the opportunity to change their destiny, so they struggled. They despised peasants and businessmen and admired the upper class. They devoted all their life to enter the upper class. There was one way to gain that. That was to enter the imperial court through examination. They also had a dream for marriage. But different from peasants, they wanted a decent, gentle and elegant woman. A Chinese poem can tell the dream precisely: the most wonderful moment in life was when newly enrolled by the imperial court and your beautiful bride right beside you.

When these Chinese became members of the intellectuals of the upper class, their dreams became bigger as well. They wanted to contribute to the country and honor their family.

This Chinese dream lasted all through the feudal society of China. With strong Chinese characteristics and Confucian ideas, it is considered as a typical Chinese dream which has its impact even in today's Chinese society.

Then came the period of foreign invasion into China. I'm afraid at that time all common Chinese people had only one dream at the bottom of their hearts: peace and a China that was strong enough to protect its people.

Now, peace finally comes and a strong China is on its way. In the new era, with the fast development of economy, Chinese people no longer worry about food. They have time and space to dream their own dreams. Affected by the globalization, facing millions of dazzling choices, the Chinese dream becomes a dream of the individual. Ask ten people in the street, you will get ten different dreams.

However, the core of the Chinese dream is still there: family. It is extremely dominant in the country. Even those in the mid- and upper class, who are greatly influenced by the western values and emphasize more of individual and freedom, are considering family life as the most important. Marrying the one you love, respecting your parents and educating your children are still the basis of the Chinese dream. On this basis, other dreams can grow and yield fruits.

Money Means Happiness?

"I've been rich and I've been poor," said actress Mae West. "Believe me, rich is better." Is that absolutely true? Everyone feels more comfortable with a certain amount of money in the bank — saving for a rainy day. Now some researchers in the United States contend that money, in fact, can buy happiness, and they know exactly how much. "It will take $1.5 million to move you from a point where you're unhappy to a point where you're happy," says one of the authors of the study. But I don't agree with them. I think if money can buy happiness, they must misunderstand the nature of happiness.

In China, there are also some statistics trying to find out the relationship between money and happiness. One of the latest statistics shows that the poor in China are not happy, but the rich in China are also not happy; the happiest people in China are the middle class. Undoubtedly, poor doesn't mean happiness, but fortune doesn't either. Happiness is based on money to a certain extent, but not the full extent. Happiness is both physical and spiritual.

When we talk about the nature of happiness, we must distinguish between happiness and fun. Many intelligent people still equate happiness with fun. The truth is that fun and happiness have little or nothing in common. Fun is what we experience during an act. Happiness is what we experience after an act. It is a deeper, more abiding emotion. Take the super stars for examples; these rich, beautiful individuals have constant access to glamorous parties, fancy cars and expensive homes; everything that spells "happiness." But celebrities often reveal the unhappiness hidden beneath all their fun: depression, alcoholism, drug addiction, broken marriage, troubled children, profound loneliness.

I think happiness should not be ideal and abstract but realistic and concrete. Maybe ordinary happiness is the ultimate happiness. We had better cherish it. Those forms of fun do not contribute in any real way to real happiness. More difficult endeavors — learning, raising children, creating a deep relationship with family members, trying to do good in the world — will bring me more happiness than can ever be found in fun, that least permanent of things. Happiness is different from fun; maybe fun has something to do with the money you own and spend, but happiness is different.

The moment we understand that fun and money do not bring happiness, we begin to lead our lives differently. The effect can be, quite literally, life-transforming. If you have a happy family where you can enjoy the family relationships and rest comfortably whenever you feel physically or psychologically tired; if you have a favorite job that gives you a stable income and you can enjoy a sense of achievement fully; if your parents are healthy and have a happy old age, you live a happy life undoubtedly, whether you are rich or not!

Private Cars: Not the More the Better

With the standard of living rising, more and more people in China now have their own cars, and as a result of China's entering WTO, the price of both domestic and imported cars has decreased a lot, which makes more people join the queue to buy cars. Many people believe that private cars can greatly improve the quality of living; some of them even look forward to the day when each family in China has at least a car, claiming it is a sign of prosperity, but, is that really so? Look deeper into this issue, we will find it is not as simple as we may think. A series of problems can arise from the ever many private cars.

First, as we all know, China has the largest population in the world. If each family owns at least one car, it will be a colossal number. With so many cars running on the not so wide roads, what will be the result? There will be far more traffic jams, long queues of luxurious private cars waiting on the roads, with their owners anxiously, even furiously, yet powerlessly being stuck in the cars. In this way, even the very first wish of having private cars — being convenient — cannot be guaranteed. It may turn out that it takes much more time than before when we traveled by bus. What's more, you cannot expect a driver to be in a good mood if there are so many traffic jams, and emotion can affect driving, weakening their capacity of judging correctly, which eventually will bring about more traffic accidents.

Second, more private cars certainly require more parking lots. But considering the rare and precious earth, especially in some big cities like Beijing, Shanghai, or Shenzhen, where nearly every inch of land has already been used fully, it is impossible to build parking lots in large scales. Then imagine the frustration of car-owners when they get to the destination in time only to find that there is no parking space, and after they find a space and park their cars properly, they may be late for a very important meeting. On the other hand, as parking lots are not enough, parking fees will inevitably go up, which should be added to the cost of maintaining a private car.

Third, too many private cars definitely will add fuel to the environmental pollution as well as the energy crisis. Before we usually boasted of our extended land and rich resources, but now we come to realize that China is not a country rich in energy or resources, especially when taking its large population into consideration. That's why the government has been advocating sustainable economic development. Although there have emerged some cars that use solar power or electricity power, they are just experimental innovations, and it will be a long time before these kinds of "clean" cars can be put into production and come to the hands of ordinary consumers. So at present, one of the effective ways to reduce the air pollution caused by cars and soften the energy crisis is to control the number of cars.

Anyhow, we should judge the issue of private cars from China's own special situation. China is a country with a huge population and comparatively rare resources. Too many private cars can only make the traffic worse, bring about more accidents, increase the environment and energy problem. Besides, the price of cars is not as cheap as many people thought after taking other expenses into account, such as parking fees and gasoline costs. There may develop a phenomenon that you can afford to buy a car but not maintain a car, which means that having a private car cannot give the owner the pleasure that he thought he should have enjoyed. So, I think what we should do is to make more efforts to improve our public transportation system, to attract more people to travel by bus, by underground, and other public means, rather than advocating people to buy their own cars.

The Sun and the Sunflower

It is only a couple of days ago that I saw a Chinese movie called "The Sunflower under the Sunshine." It tells a story about a father and a son. The sunflower appears in the whole movie and becomes the image of animate life. It also represents the son, of course. The sun represents the father. The sunflower just gets sunshine from the sun all day long, never tries to understand it. Although the sun is fervent and awful, the sunflower will follow it. Actually the "sun" expresses his love in this way to the sunflower without saying anything. After the movie, I didn't do anything but to think about my father for a very long time.

In my memory, my father is a stalwart man, and a very handsome man. He has a pair of big eyes and a couple of bushy, black eyebrows. His hands are so big and powerful that he can pick me up with one hand easily before I was seven. He is always kind to everyone and always smiles to everyone. However, there is one exception, that is me. When I was small, he forced me to learn the violin. He did not let me play with other children. To play the violin and to study is the only thing I can do. Just before I saw the movie, "father" is a representative of power, rigorousness, and a man without a smile. I am so scared of him that I even do not want to speak to him. But the movie aroused me, something happened between father and me.

About one year ago, I broke up with my first boyfriend. I was so depressed that I did not say a word in 3 days. At that time, my mother was not at home and I could feel my father's anxiousness, but I still did not want to talk to him. On the fourth day's morning, I found a piece of paper on my desk: "The art of life is to know how to enjoy it, not to bear it. Everyday, should give you a little confidence. Although you have 1000 reasons to make you cry, you should have 1001 reasons to make you smile." I knew it was written by my father. I saw his bloodshot eyes, and then, I was a little moved, a kind of warm feeling went around me.

Now, I can clearly see everything my father did for me. Father uses his way to love me. He did all he could to love me. I could not see what he did for me, but I can feel it. Love without words, still powerful, just like the love between the sun and sunflower.

I plan to give this movie to my father. When the movie is finished I want to tell him that I love him, always.

Bibliography

An Xin. "Growing Up Story (in Chinese)." *China Youth*, October 2005.

Barnett, A. Doak. *China's Far West: Four Decades of Change*. Boulder, CO: Westview Press, 1993.

Becker, Jasper. "China's Growing Pains." *National Geographic*, March 2004.

Beech, Hannah. "Enemies of the State." *Time*, September 19, 2005.

Ch'ien Chung-shu. *Fortress Besieged*. Translated by Jeanne Kelly and Nathan K. Mao. Beijing: Foreign Language Teaching and Research Press, 2003. Originally published, 1947.

China Daily newspaper, 2005–2007.

China Daily online, 2006–2007.

China Handbook Editorial Committee. *Education and Science*. Beijing: China Handbook Series, 1983.

Deng, Benjamin. *Deng: A Political Biography*. Armonk, NY: M.E. Sharpe, 1998.

Deng Xiaoping. *Selected Works of Deng Xiaoping (1975–1982)*. Translated version. Beijing: Foreign Languages Press, 1984.

Ding Zuxin. *An Anthology of Chinese Poetry*. Shenyang: Liaoning University Press, 1995.

Gao, James Zheng. *The Communist Takeover of Hangzhou: The Transformation of City and Cadre, 1949–1954*. Honolulu: University of Hawaii Press, 2004.

Gernet, Jacques. *Daily Life in China on the Eve of the Mongol Invasion 1250–1276*. Originally written in French. Translated. New York: Macmillan, 1962.

Han, Dongping. *The Unknown Cultural Revolution: Educational Reforms and Their Impact on China's Rural Development*. New York: Garland Publishing, 2000.

Han Suyin. *Eldest Son: Zhou Enlai and the Making of Modern China 1898–1976*. New York: Hill & Wang, division of Farrar, Straus and Giroux, 1994.

History and Civilization of China. Beijing: CIP, 2003.

Hu Jintao. "President of China Visits Yale." *Yale Bulletin & Calendar*. New Haven, CT, May 5, 2006.

International Institute for Applied Systems Analysis (IIASA) Website. Laxenburg: Austria.

Kuhn, Robert Lawrence. *The Man Who Changed China: The Life and Legacy of Jiang Zemin*. New York: Crown, 2004.

Li Haibo. "Will Egalitarianism Return?" *Beijing Review*. March 31, 2005.

Lo, C.P., and Xiao-Di Song. "Ningbo: East China's Rising Industrial Port." In *China's Coastal Cities*. Edited by Yue-man Yeung and Xu-wei Hu. Honolulu: University of Hawaii Press, 1992.

Lorenz, Andreas. "The Chinese Miracle Will End Soon." *Der Spiegel* online. March 7, 2005.

Lu Xun. *Call to Arms.* Translated by Yang Xianyi and Gladys Yang. Beijing: Foreign Languages Press, 2000.

Mao Dun. *The Shop of the Lin Family & Spring Silkworms.* Translated by Sidney Shapiro. Hong Kong: The Chinese University Press, 2004. Original Chinese publication, 1932.

Peking Review. October 29, 1976.

PEP Primary English Students' Book. Beijing: Lingo Media and People's Education Press, 2003.

Polo, Marco. *The Travels of Marco Polo.* Translated by Teresa Waugh. New York: Facts on File, 1984.

Polo, Marco. *The Travels of Marco Polo.* Everyman's Library. New York: E.P. Dutton, 1908.

Schultheis, Eugenia Barnett. *Hangchow, My Home: Growing up in Heaven Below.* Fort Bragg, CA: Lost Coast Press, 2000.

Seckington, Ian. "Who's Hu?" *China Review Magazine* 21 (2002).

Senior English for China Student's Book 1B. Beijing: People's Education Press, 2003.

Shao Bin. *New English Words Show.* Dalian: Dalian University of Technology Press, 2006.

Snow, Edgar. *The Other Side of the River: Red China Today.* New York: Random House, 1961.

Stuart, John Leighton. *Fifty Years in China: The Memoirs of John Leighton Stuart.* New York: Random House, 1954.

Su Wenming, ed. *A Nation at School.* Beijing: Beijing Review Special Feature Series, 1983.

Waley, Arthur. *Chinese Poems.* London: Unwin Books, 1961.

Wang, Xiufang. *Education in China since 1976.* Jefferson, NC: McFarland, 2003.

Wen Jiabao. "Remarks of Chinese Premier Wen Jiabao." *Harvard Gazette*, December 12, 2003.

Yu Xiangjun. "Living with Films." *China Today* (September 2005).

Yuhuan county, Zhejiang province, China, Website.

Index

Affiliated Primary School of Zhejiang University 156, 160–163
Africa 42, 87, 96, 99
Alice 108, 121–129, 174
An Xin 17, 29, 30, 32, 83–102, 178, 184
Anhui province 14, 15, 16, 29, 32, 44, 61–82, 117, 155, 159–160, 187

Bai Juyi 9
Beijing 7, 13, 32, 45–50, 83, 85, 89, 90, 92, 94, 97, 98, 102, 104, 113, 137, 138, 139, 146, 153, 162, 167, 175, 183, 188, 190
bound feet 88, 141
Buddhism 7, 72, 81–82, 89, 90, 94, 175

Carson, Rachel 122,
Chen, Xue-Qun 18, 131–138, 147, 174
Chiang Kai-shek 13, 14
Christianity 7, 10, 11, 93, 113, 114, 175
Cindy 148, 156–159
Comfort, Alex 67
communes 15, 16, 21, 58, 71, 81
Communist Party of China (CCP) 6, 13, 19, 23, 96, 97, 182, 189, 190, 191
Confucianism 9, 11, 89, 111, 168, 175, 186, 189, 193
Cultural Revolution 19–22, 23, 25, 30, 40, 43, 44, 54, 55, 75, 81, 87, 104, 130, 141, 143, 148, 149, 150, 174, 182

Daguan Middle School 156, 163–165
Dalian 118, 119, 121, 131, 132
Deng Xiaoping 13, 23, 24, 25, 26, 61, 67, 126, 164, 175, 190
Deqing Vocational School 156, 165–167, 182
Du, Ji-Zeng 136, 137

Eliot, George 92, 94, 97, 101
England 144–146, 147, 174

Epstein, Israel 84
Evelyn 18, 20, 32, 33–39, 179

Fan Gao 16, 31, 32, 61–75, 101, 155, 159, 178
Feng Zikai 115, 117
Fortress Besieged 67

Gansu province 18, 133–135, 190
Gernet, Jacques 10
Grand Canal 7, 8
Great Leap Forward 15, 16, 54, 80
Guilin 92, 94, 101
Guizhou province 14, 95, 153, 191

Haley, Alex 58, 122
Han, Dongping 19, 21, 22, 23
Hangzhou 5, 6, 7–11, 18, 32, 33–39, 78, 86, 89, 92, 93, 94, 95, 102, 103, 109, 112, 114, 119, 120, 136, 142, 147, 156, 162, 163, 165
Hangzhou University 11, 112, 113, 150
Hardy, Thomas 78
Hefei 29, 61, 62, 77, 147, 184
Hemingway, Ernest 101, 129
Henan province 13, 15, 16, 53, 55, 182
Hong Kong 26, 37, 92, 138, 146
household responsibility system 25, 58, 63, 187
Hu Jintao 6, 18, 23, 26, 104, 188, 189, 190–192
Hua Guo-feng 23
Hughes, Langston 45
Hunan province 57–61, 133
hutong 46–48

Ian 22, 140–148, 155, 156, 157, 159, 174
Inner Mongolia Autonomous Region 50, 183

199

iron rice bowl system 58
Islam 7, 89

Japan 13, 14, 17, 43, 54, 104, 141, 176, 180
Jiang Zemin 23, 191
Jilin province 44, 139, 140

Kissinger, Henry 22
Korean War 17, 54
Kuomintang (KMT) 13, 14, 20, 40, 54, 80

Lanzhou 133–135, 136, 137
Los Angeles 37, 38, 39
Loudi 60
Lu, Xun 91, 111
Lynd, Robert and Helen 123

Mao Dun 78, 143
Mao Zedong 12, 13, 14, 15, 19, 22, 50, 54, 57, 61, 67, 81, 84, 87, 90, 103, 108, 133, 150, 155, 174, 185
Marx, Karl 67, 144, 145, 174
migrant worker 73, 124, 153, 176
Ming dynasty 62, 67, 89
Mouse 69–70

Nanjing 13, 70, 135, 147
Nearing, Scott and Helen 123
Needham, Joseph 14
Ningbo 141–143, 150
Nixon, Richard 22, 143

one-child policy 26, 55, 58, 65, 108, 115, 127, 128, 130, 159, 166, 185–187

Packard, Vance 123
Pan Yue 183, 184
Peking opera 42, 48
Polo, Marco 7, 9, 10

Qian Yi 99, 184
Qiantang River 10
Qing dynasty 11, 48, 62, 67

Red Army 13, 14, 54, 80, 84

Schultheis, Eugenia Barnett 10, 11
Shaanxi province 14, 83–92
Shang dynasty 51
Shanghai 6, 7, 13, 20, 39–45, 73, 91, 121, 142, 144, 167, 179, 189
Shao Bin 108, 115–121, 174

Shaoxing 109, 111, 112, 113
Shaoxing opera 42, 125, 176
Shirley 17, 108, 109–115, 174, 186
silk 7, 18, 34, 35, 89
Sinclair, Upton 78
Singapore 52
Snow, Edgar 51
Song dynasty 7, 9, 89
The Sound of Music 91, 128
Soviet Union 17, 18, 133
Stuart, John Leighton 10
Su Shi 9
Sunnie 32, 45–50
Suzhou 9, 121

Taiwan 6, 14, 20, 26
Tan, Amy 78, 100
Tang dynasty 9, 65, 89, 141
Taoism 7, 148, 159
tea 7, 95, 96
Thousand Island Lake 17, 111, 117
Tianjin 91, 99, 134, 135, 136, 137, 180
Tibet 139–140, 191
traditional Chinese medicine 74, 75, 134, 135, 137, 152, 178
Tsinghua University 92, 97, 98, 99, 102, 184, 190
Twain, Mark 68

UNESCO 63, 99
United Nations 22, 190
University of California, Los Angeles (UCLA) 38

Vermont 8, 9, 161, 162
Vivian 15, 18, 50–56

Weiqiu 159–160, 186
Wen Jiabao 6, 18, 179, 181, 187
Wendy 32, 57–61
Wenzhou 123, 124, 125
West Lake 8, 9, 12, 21, 78, 79, 86, 102, 115, 147
William 19, 20, 39–45
Wood, Benjamin 8
World War II 13, 43, 53–54, 95
Wuyue kingdom 7

Xi'an 32, 75, 83, 84, 85, 88–92
Xi'an International Studies University 29
Xianyang 32, 83–88, 184
Xin'an River Hydropower station 17, 111

Xinjiang Uygur Autonomous Region 49, 183, 188
Xue Yan 14, 15, 16, 29, 32, 61–62, 75–82, 101

Yale University 6, 18, 26, 100, 190, 192
Yang, li-qiu 138–140
Yangtze River 6, 19, 27, 141, 184, 192
Yellow Mountain 62, 63, 64, 65, 73, 160, 187
Yellow River 51, 84, 133, 134
Yuan dynasty 47
Yuhuan county 124–129

Zhejiang Normal University 126–127
Zhejiang province 6, 7, 20, 34, 44, 108, 111, 117, 122, 124, 139, 141, 142, 156, 166, 173, 185
Zhejiang University 5, 7, 11–12, 14, 22, 27, 29–32, 92, 93, 95, 101, 103, 107, 108, 109, 113, 114, 123, 136, 137, 140, 144, 145, 146, 147, 149, 160; Yuquan campus 12, 14, 132; Zhijiang University 11, 93, 94, 144; Zijingang campus 11, 30, 31, 69, 77, 93, 131
Zhejiang University of Finance and Economics 108, 113, 116, 119, 120, 121, 156
Zhengzhou 18, 51–56
Zhou Enlai 17, 22, 96
Zhu Kezhen 12
Zunyi 14, 95